Master Storytelling:

How to Turn Your Experiences into Stories that Teach, Lead, and Inspire

Mark Carpenter ✦ Darrell Harmon

Copyright © 2018 Mindset Strategic Leadership and Circo Şolo
All rights reserved.
ISBN-13: 9781724199218

In a Nutshell

Foreword by Ron McMillan	1
Preamble: Whose Line is it?	5
Introduction: Why Stories Rule	6
1. Stories Matter Because …	14
2. Use Stories to …	30
3. You Can Find Stories …	49
4. Great Stories Include …	62
5. How Can Questions Help?	86
6. Finish Your Story by …	108
Appendix: Story Examples	134
Endnotes (citations and other confessions)	163
Who are These Guys?	168

Foreword

I left my home a week ago and traveled to a city I hadn't heard of until I read my itinerary. I traveled by car, plane, and bus. When I arrived, I was amazed! I was shocked! I fell in love.

Hmmm, perhaps I should add more detail to my story. I am a well-traveled American. I travel for business and pleasure and have been to more places than most people I know. I consider myself well-informed about people and places. Yet, as I write this story, I am in a city I have never before visited. In fact, I hadn't even heard of this place, nor heard its name spoken. As part of a six-city trip, I arrived this morning and was instantly smitten.

This city lies between two beautiful rivers that meet near the city center and flow on to become a major tributary of the third longest river on Earth. There are 36 bridges in the city, which enable the millions of residents to get around using cars, trucks, trains, buses, and even miles and miles of a new monorail system.

Have you guessed the city yet? I bet you haven't.

There are thousands of high-rises and marvelous, new business buildings. They have high-tech companies, heavy manufacturing, even huge car manufacturing centers that make Fords, Hondas, Toyotas, and many other brands.

Everywhere there is evidence of great wealth. International companies have invested billions in advertisements, showrooms, and stores, including Gucci, BMW, and Tiffani's. I walked a downtown intersection crammed with thousands of people that surpasses New York's Times Square or London's Piccadilly Circus in terms of hustle and bustle, vibrant shoppers, giant video screens, and pulsating music.

Also, this city is populated by over 53 significant minority groups.

I was amazed. Why had I never heard of this place before? Do you know where I am now? Need more clues?

In a verdant tangle of exotic trees and flowers is a fabulous park that has an incredible zoo with local, well-cared-for animals, some of which I've never heard of nor even seen pictures of before. Thrilling!

Okay, if this doesn't give it away, then you're probably like me: a well-informed, slightly arrogant, but still curious explorer who is surprised by learning something new about a topic I previously thought I was proficient in.

I discovered that (depending on which Internet site you care to believe) this is the most populous city in the world! (It may be second to Mexico City, depending on where you draw the city limits.)

How could I not know about this wonderful city before now? This is absolutely thrilling! I have discovered a fabulous new city to explore! Exciting!

Now, howsabout we take this little travel story and apply it to you and your life? Perhaps there are some exciting, profitable discoveries waiting for you.

Consider your expertise and experience. Perhaps you are a trainer, teacher, leader, co-worker, parent, or a volunteer neighborhood dog leavings clean-up person. Think about the roles in your life that require you to interact with others. What if, with all that knowledge you possess about dealing with others, there were an area of knowledge and skill that you didn't know about—like me and my new favorite city? What if knowing more about this area could dramatically and powerfully increase your effectiveness with others? Would you want to know about it? Understand it? Use it to improve your outcomes and relationships?

I predict that this book, *Master Storytelling: How to Turn Your Experiences into Stories that Teach, Lead and Inspire*, will surprise you like the unknown city surprised me. I suspect you know a lot about storytelling. You've heard stories and told them your whole life. Get ready for an amazing surprise!

Mark Carpenter and Darrell Harmon have discovered how this well-recognized form of communication can be deeply utilized to improve your interactions in powerful ways. Through the effective use of well-prepared stories, data dumps or boring meetings can be turned into inspiring, memorable, motivating experiences. But the authors don't stop at announcing you "oughta wanna" tell stories; they teach you how. Mark and Darrell take you through a step-by-step process that helps you create focused stories that work.

Their book teaches you the skill of turning life experiences into stories that teach, lead, and inspire. It isn't about simply relating an experience; it's crafting your experiences into effective stories that move other people to action.

I enthusiastically recommend this book to you. It will make an important difference.

And, just in case you haven't yet figured it out, my "unknown city" is Chongqing, the most populous city in China with over 33 million people. Be sure to Google "red panda" and "white tigers."

Ron McMillan, four-time *New York Times* best-selling author, including *Crucial Conversations: Tools for Talking When Stakes Are High*

Preamble: Whose Line is it?

It's a little tricky to co-author a book and make the voice sound consistent. Mark and Darrell each wrote different sections of this book and then added to the other's sections. We then discussed everything and came to agreement on all of it, so we speak with a single voice. Whatever Darrell says, Mark says. Whatever Mark says, Darrell says.

When we share a personal experience (and, of course, we share *lots* of them), we simply say, "I ..." and then tell the story. We didn't think it was important to identify who was speaking. We'll let you guess. We chose this convention primarily for ease in reading. (You're welcome.) We didn't want to use clunky verbiage like, "When one of us was ..." or "Mark/Darrell had an experience ...." Our focus is on the story, because the hero is the story, not the storyteller.

Ready? Here's the first one ...

Introduction: Why Stories Rule

I once worked for a small survey company that was trying to grow into an organizational development consultancy, but we were having a hard time getting traction. Each time we administered a customized survey measuring, say, employee engagement, we would deliver the results to the executive team of the client organization. We provided reports with bounteous color-coded charts and graphs, slicing and dicing the data from an assortment of perspectives. We then finished triumphantly with a flourish of recommendations. (If you've worked in a corporation of any size, this ritual should sound familiar.) But all too often, after the presentation, the executive team members would thank us for our work and then rush off to another meeting (or so they said).

Hmmm, this isn't working.

So, one day, back at the office, several of us played the role of executive team for a mock presentation done by two of our best consultants. They knew the numbers inside and out. They could tell us if a score in the 75th percentile was acceptable or portended the imminent exit of key employees. Our "executive team" was to assess the effectiveness of the presentation and see if we could find ways to increase up-selling opportunities.

As I sat through the presentation, I became increasingly bored—and concerned. While my colleagues did a stellar job of reporting the survey findings, they did nothing to help me want to care about the results. These were bright, motivated (even animated) people, but the more they talked, the less I wanted to listen.

The problem was not their intellect or their understanding of survey numbers, or even their earnestness. It was their approach presenting the numbers. They seemed to think that if they thoroughly explained how skillfully they had surveyed the employees and how excited they were about what the numbers told them, I'd want to hire them to do follow-up work. I should see what they saw and care about what they cared about in the numbers.

But I didn't.

It then dawned on me that what we needed—both the presenters and the audience—was an entirely different approach, one that would allow the consultants to share their insights in a way that made sense to the audience and addressed *their* needs. Instead of just reporting the findings and giving some interpretation of how good or bad they were, we needed to talk to our clients in terms of daily life within their organization. We needed to paint a picture of the frustration their employees felt after six months on the job when the thrill of their new role had worn off and it was now the same old, same old, day in and day out. They weren't learning anything new and were starting to go numb between the ears. We needed to tell our clients why marketing team members and accounting staff had such vastly different scores on finding meaning in their work, and what that meant for retention. We needed to vividly portray what their employees were trying to say through the survey's five-point scale. But all the presenters did was report 4.7, 3.2, 4.3, and 2.9. So what?

They needed to tell us the *story* of the numbers.

I realized that our clients weren't just paying us to run a survey and then give them an expert's view of the numbers. They wanted our color commentary in addition to our colored charts. They wanted to know what the numbers had to say about the things they, as leaders, cared about most: Are their employees going to stick around another year or are they updating their resumes? How could they unleash their employees' passion for their work? What could they do to stimulate more innovative ideas to keep their organization competitive? Where were our answers to *those* questions?

In answering those questions, we needed to give the employees a voice. Of course, we wouldn't name specific people, but we could create archetypes of the different "employees" we were seeing in the numbers: those who were happy, those who wished things would change, and those who were on the doorstep heading out of the building. We should amalgamate the data, then shape the results into narratives that would represent the employees' feedback and speak to the executives.

We should tell their stories.

Storytelling is *sense-making*. It goes well beyond just reporting facts. Stories connect the dots and help us understand the importance of the facts, how those facts affect us. Stories involve people and situations we can relate to, so we understand *and feel* the meaning of the experience we're reporting. When we relate to a story, we insert ourselves into it and it comes to life for us. Facts and figures then take on color, contour, and significance. As actor and author Alan Alda points out, "We listen better to a story. We get involved when we hear a story." That's sense-making.

The epiphany I had about our executive presentations illustrates a challenge most of us have in our lives: How do we move others to meaningful action? How do we sell our ideas, whether we're in the classroom, the boardroom, or the break room? Whether we're trying to illustrate the need for safety compliance, demonstrate the value of an idea we want backing for, or show a prospective employer that we're the perfect candidate for the job, how do we convince others to buy into our ideas? How do we connect our ideas to their needs in a way that is meaningful and impactful to them? This is where stories can make the difference.

Whether we realize it or not, stories are an integral part of our human experience. Consider this: Humans have only used written communication for about 10,000 years (give or take a century). But as a species, we've been telling each other stories from the very beginning, and we continue to use them for an array of purposes.

There are many different kinds of stories: fairy tales (the "Once upon a time ..." kind), movies and novels of different genres, professional presentations, stand-up routines, political and marketing pitches (often unintentionally similar to stand-up routines in their effect if not their intent), and others. They differ in their forms and communication media, but they typically share some common objectives: to inform, convey values, entertain, make a point and, above all, *move us*. To do that, they often have some sort of storyline—set-up, action, conclusion—and they have interesting, relatable characters.

Here's an example:

An 80-year-old woman gets arrested for shoplifting. When she goes before the judge he asks her, "Ma'am, what did you steal?"

She replies: "A can of peaches."

The judge asks, "Why did you steal a can of peaches?"

"Because I was hungry, Your Honor," the woman replies.

"Well, ma'am," the judge asks, "just how many peaches were in that can?"

"Only six, Your Honor," she replies pitifully.

"Six peaches, huh?" the judge repeats. He then says, "All right, for stealing six peaches I sentence you to six days in jail."

Before the judge could finish pronouncing the punishment, however, the old woman's husband speaks up and asks the judge if he could say something.

"Yes, sir," the judge says. "What is it?"

The husband says, "She also stole a can of peas."

But seriously, folks . . .

While jokes are fun, we would argue that some of the best uses of stories are to *teach*, *lead*, and *inspire*. This book is our attempt to help you do that better, whatever your role, whatever your situation.

There are many ways we typically try to teach, lead, and inspire: We share data (loooots of data), pour enthusiasm into rah-rah pep talks, create campaign slogans (with swag for emphasis), shout dire warnings, show flashy-splashy graphics, etc.—all to get our message across. While those can have some impact, stories are an often-underutilized tool that can add power to our efforts. But we're not talking about creating epic movies, YouTube videos, hilarious stand-up bits, or best-selling novels. We think there's great power in using your everyday experiences to drive home the points you're trying to make in brief but well-crafted stories. Your anecdotes can lead others to take action.

A Sneak Peek

In the following pages we'll share ideas, examples, recommendations, and practice suggestions for honing your storytelling skills. We'll give you insights into why our brains light up when we hear a great story. We'll also show you practical ways to take slices of your "ordinary" life (as if there were such a thing) and transform them into a memorable and persuasive tool for moving others willingly to purposeful action. Whether you're a natural storyteller or have never considered stories as a tool you could use, you'll find helpful information in this book. We believe that the simple skills of storytelling will be a revelation—and maybe a revolution—in your life.

Each chapter will conclude with a *summary of main points* and an *application section*. You'll be collecting useful ideas throughout the chapter, and by the end you'll be itching to put them to good use. So, grab your favorite writing utensil (paper and pen, laptop, tablet, or quill and parchment) and get ready to capture insights, bolts of inspiration, and application ideas. You also have the option of using our specially-crafted Story Catcher, which you can find on our website at www.Master-Storytelling.com. We'll unleash your storytelling superpower bit by bit as you make your way through the book. The story catcher will help you catch ideas as they pop into your head, then lead you through the process of turning your real-life experiences into stories that teach, lead, and inspire.

We're glad you've chosen to take this journey with us. Let's get started.

One: Stories Matter Because …

In 2009, *New York Times* columnist Rob Walker and author Josh Glenn bought a couple of hundred trinkets from thrift stores and garage sales, paying about $1.25 apiece, on average, for the lot. Next, they hired writers to create fictitious stories about each item. The stuff then went on eBay, with a picture of each item paired with its fabricated story in lieu of a straightforward description. Walker and Glenn believed the stories would increase the trinkets' market value by imbuing them with an apparent increased worth.

What do you think happened?

The objects were purchased for a total of $250, yet sold for nearly $8,000 — an increase of around 3100%!

Walker and Glenn called their experiment the Significant Objects Project, hypothesizing that they could take items of little value and elevate them to significance by injecting them with meaning through a story. It worked.[1]

For example, the story by three-time *Jeopardy!* champion Doug Dorst about a figurine of "St.

Vralkomir" catapulted the statuette's original sale price of $3 to a whopping $193.50, an increase of 6350%! Kate Bernheimer bested that by writing a tragic tale about a kitschy pink toy horse and vaulting its price from $1 to $104.50, or 10,450%. The guys were onto something here.

As Duke University psychology and behavioral economics professor Dan Ariely explains, "The results may seem surprising, but this is actually something we see all the time. It's the basic idea behind the 'endowment effect,' the theory that once we own something, its value increases in our eyes."[2] The fictions written about each item created in the minds of buyers a kind of ownership they would not have otherwise felt, and for which they were willing to pay handsomely.

The stories were so powerful that they lifted the perceived value of this collection of bric-a-brac exponentially. The kicker is that none of the stories accompanying the items was true! This fact was not hidden, but buyers were so enamored with the stories that the fabricated descriptions sparked buyers' imaginations and increased the value of the things associated with them. That's because we buy *meaning*, not stuff. We buy feelings like hope and love and what-if that tickle our fancy. This is the currency of the heart and mind.

Don Hewitt, creator of the perennially successful television newsmagazine *60 Minutes*, understood this and had a simple approach to vetting potential ideas for a new segment on the show. When someone would come into his office and begin pitching an idea, Don would hold up his hand and say, "Wait a minute. Four words: Tell me a story." He felt that storytelling was the key to making *60 Minutes* successful. He was no doubt right.[3]

The Power in Stories

So, what is it about stories that captivates us? Several things come into play that help stories grab us by the ears — and minds and hearts — and make us listen, learn, and feel. In brief, stories are how we think. They're how we experience life. They're natural to us. Anecdotes combine colorful snippets of real life, bathed in irresistible emotions.

Neuroeconomist Dr. Paul Zak[4] has studied the brain chemistry involved with stories and has found that they trigger the release of certain chemicals in our brains. Specifically, oxytocin and cortisol levels are elevated when we're enraptured by a story.

Oxytocin increases our empathy and feelings of emotional safety. It's what Zak calls the "trust hormone." It tells us that it's safe to approach a person or enter a story. In short, stories fast-track trust.

C*ortisol*, on the other hand, increases our focus and attention, which is why we can feel transported from our here-and-now reality to a there-and-then state, placing us mentally within the story and making it irresistible. We take the journey with the storyteller. We can't resist.

Additionally, when we tell stories we can trigger a nice hit of *dopamine*, a neurotransmitter connected to the brain's reward system. Dopamine, like oxytocin, makes us feel good. It's released in anticipation of a reward, as well as when we finally receive the reward. As soon as we anticipate that the "goal" of the story will be reached we get a hit of dopamine. Then, when it *is* reached, we get a second hit of dopamine. Yummy! (More later on how to stimulate these brain states as storytellers.)

So, why the biology lesson in a book about storytelling? Well-told stories trigger emotions in our audience and chemically change them. Stories transform bland bullet points into moments of meaning and motivation. Stories make our data dynamic and move our audience to action.

But wait, there's more.

Neuroscience researcher Dr. Giacomo Rizzolatti[5] and his colleagues discovered something curious while observing macaque monkeys that may give us insight into why we find stories so irresistible. The researchers noted that the monkeys' brains seemed to be sympathetic to the actions of the researchers. That is, when one of the researchers reached for a piece of fruit in front of the monkey, the part of the monkey's brain that reaches for fruit lit up! Note that it was not the part of the monkey's brain that *observes* someone reaching for fruit, but the part that activates when the monkey itself *actually reaches* for fruit. It was as if the monkey itself were acting rather than just observing. Huh! Rizzolatti and his colleagues dubbed these *mirror neurons*, because they are neurons that mirror the actions of others.

According to Dr. Marco Iaconobi[6] at UCLA, we humans go one step further, and this just might draw a clearer distinction between us and lower primates (your brother-in-law notwithstanding). Not only do our motor neurons fire when observing what someone does—what the scientists call the *goal*—but humans also intuitively understand *how* the goal is achieved and *why*. This is key to imitation: We don't merely duplicate the accomplishment of someone else's goal (i.e., copy their actions), but we understand how they did it and what their reasons were. These are then transferred to us.

This explains why yawns can be so contagious. When you yawn, my brain picks up a signal that I should want to yawn too—and, of course, I know how you did that and how to do it myself. It's nearly automatic. This also applies for higher-level activities, like those we tell stories about: learning to resolve conflict, reframing inexperience as a job-related advantage, or persuading a CEO to act ethically. (You can read examples of these kinds of stories in the appendix.)

Well, what do monkey brains, picking up fruit, and yawning have to do with the power of stories? When you tell a story with a plotline and characters that I can relate to, I respond on multiple levels. Not only do I understand *what* you're telling me (cognitive level), I place myself *within* your story and *feel* it (emotional level). I access my own storehouse of experiences and my mirror neurons make your story *mine*, pretty vividly if not literally. And when we feel ownership for something, we value it more and are reluctant to let it go — the "endowment effect" that we cited earlier. When we own it, it tends to move us. That's why stories grab us so tightly.

To take this one step further, fMRI research at Princeton led by Uri Hasson has shown that when someone tells us an engaging story our brains synchronize with the storyteller's brain patterns. As we begin to listen to the story, our brain activity follows slightly *behind* the teller's brain. But as the story continues and we become engrossed in it, our brains catch up and synchronize with the storyteller's brain and we walk step-for-step through the story with the narrator. Eventually, if the story is similar to one we ourselves have experienced, our brains actually fire *ahead* of the teller's brain! We experience this as, "Oh, I see where this is going!" and start to *anticipate* the next part of the story. We become enmeshed in it, tracking all its twists and turns.

This is what stimulates the release of oxytocin and cortisol during the story and sets us up for a nice hit of dopamine when we finally arrive at the happy ending. It's also what sets us up for a surprise (and another hit of cortisol) when the story takes a sudden and dramatic turn: "Whoa, I did *not* see that coming!"

This can also pay off for you as the storyteller by creating "social capital" for you. When your audience connects with your story and takes the journey with you, they connect to you personally. This shared experience draws them closer to you as they travel through the ups and downs of your narrative. As author Patti Digh observed, "The shortest distance between two people is a story."[7] Audience members feel drawn to *you* as they give you credit for the emotions they feel through your story. You are, in a sense, the meta-hero of the story by bringing the story to them. They attribute to you the positive feelings they get as the story unfolds and comes to resolution. Far from *shooting* the messenger, the audience praises you. They emotionally hoist you on their shoulders and celebrate what you've done for them. You are driving the dopamine train.

Storytelling: Your Superpower

The implications should now be clear. You tell me a story I can relate to and it comes alive for me. Why? Because I've experienced something similar, so my neurons fire away, making me relive my earlier experience and walk with you through yours. This virtual trip down memory lane then activates my emotional reaction to both my experience and the one you're telling me now. I'm sucked into the action of your story and feel invested in it. That's power.

But using stories as a tool to teach, lead, and inspire is more than just a feel-good experience. Stories turn a passive mental activity into an active one. The emotions that we elicit during a well-told narrative add to the cognitive charge of the story's message. People understand and remember data wrapped in stories. So, whether you're using your stories to teach a course, inspire a team, make a sale, or get a promotion, showcasing your point through a story will power it up. Stories activate the amygdala, a part of the brain near the brain's "storage unit." The vividness of the story, plus the emotional impact of it, create memorable experiences for listeners.

As Kendall Haven, author of *Story Proof: The Science Behind the Startling Power of Story,* explains:

> The elements that define story structure create context and relevance. Those elements create

motivation in the reader or listener to pay attention, process, absorb, and remember the incoming information. Research also shows that stories create a sense of belonging and identification.

Because stories motivate, they're an excellent leadership tool to energize and direct the actions of others. Our lives at work (and at home) can quickly become routine as we learn our duties and develop the skills to perform them. That's a good thing in many ways. It lowers our anxiety about doing our jobs, it increases our ability to perform well, and it leaves brain space for us to learn the next new thing and otherwise grow in new ways.

But the price we pay is boredom. Disengagement. The blahs. Stories can refresh the excitement we feel for our work. They can reinvigorate us and give us fresh commitment to do our best, to treat our tasks and interactions like they really matter—and then they will.

As four-time *New York Times* bestselling author and management expert Joseph Grenny observes:

> Fortunately, there is a lot a leader can do to help employees feel a deeper sense of motivation (and resultant satisfaction) in their work. And the first place to begin is with connection.

> Connection happens when you see past the details of a task to its human consequences. When you feel connected to the moral purpose of your work, you behave differently . . . .
>
> Leaders can maintain a lively sense of connection through storytelling. Most storytelling is brief. It involves using concrete examples that reframe a moment by personifying human consequences.
>
> People's feelings about their work are only partly about the work itself. They are equally, if not more so, about how they frame their work. Do they see what they're doing as a mindless ritual? Do they see it as empty compliance? Or do they see it as sacred duty? If you change the frame you change the feeling. And nothing changes frames faster than a story.[8]

Consider what one hospital did at an employee meeting to report progress on KPIs (key performance indicators). Instead of the typical death-by-PowerPoint presentation that uses an avalanche of numbers, graphs, and other data to convey their collective progress, they took a radically different approach. They had a recently-recovered patient stand on stage in front of everyone and recount her experience under their care.

She begins her narrative at the football game she had excitedly attended with her husband to watch their daughter perform in the marching band. Her enthusiasm quickly turns to horror, however, when she suffers a heart attack. She first describes the explosion of pain in her chest, followed by grief at the thought of leaving her family too soon. Her anxious husband and frightened daughter stand by her side, unable to help, as seconds became an eternity. The scene closes with this wife and mother succumbing to the attack amidst the wail of a siren and medical professionals scrambling to help her.

She then goes on to detail the care that hospital staff — from doctors to dieticians, nurses, housekeepers, and techs — all devote to her comfort and recovery. Every time she mentions a caregiver, the staff member comes on stage and shakes the patient's hand or gives her a hug. She relates the professional competence and caregiving procedures that staff administered during her stay in the hospital. She concludes by thanking the dozens of hospital staff — members of the audience — who played a critical role in her healing process. By this point, the stage is packed with the people who had been part of this single patient's care.

Imagine the impact *this* presentation would have had on you had you been one of the many who had treated this woman, either medically or in a support role. Whether you were the doctor who inserted catheters to open up her arteries or the housekeepers who brightened up each day by ensuring that smudges were cleaned from her windows, you would know you had made a difference. You'd be recognized alongside the nurse who responded to her craving for ice cream with a low-fat, no-sugar-added ice cream sandwich and the transport team who asked her each time they moved her if she needed an extra blanket. The patient's story would have left no doubt that you had made a difference with your day-to-day efforts at work. These are the details that matter, and they get lost in numbers and graphs. They only come alive in a story.

Research shows that one of the greatest motivators is a sense of progress toward a goal we care about.[9] So, if you're trying to inspire the troops to higher levels of performance — or just to keep going through the drudgery of their everyday work life — share a story that shows them they're making progress. Help them see that the daily grind is actually moving them closer to accomplishing an objective they care about.

As Harrison Monarth eloquently put it:

> Life happens in the narratives we tell one another. A story can go where quantitative analysis is denied admission: our hearts. Data can persuade people, but it doesn't inspire them to act; to do that, you need to wrap your vision in a story that fires the imagination and stirs the soul.[10]

All's Well . . .

A happy ending will help release oxytocin and dopamine, which produce the emotional finale you want. People will be stimulated by conflict—danger, risk, problems—but they'll then want a resolution. If you leave them hanging, or fail to connect the dots through the narrative, they won't see you as a trustworthy guide. Instead, show how you were able to overcome the odds stacked against you with the skill you're teaching, or how you should have used it. Lessons learned can be powerful as well.

Putting elements that induce oxytocin and cortisol together, we paint a picture of people our audience can relate to, and they'll insert themselves into it. We then threaten the serene scene with conflict and risk, but finally come out on the other side better for the journey. When using story as a teaching tool, the hero is the skill we employed to help us surmount the struggle and emerge victorious. As the storytellers, we are the humble guide showing how the hero saved the day.

By using stories as a teaching tool, we combine clear skill instruction with strong, positive emotions to create a memorable and enjoyable learning experience. You don't have to be a professional comedian—or even a professional storyteller—to take advantage of the multiple benefits of story. All you have to do is identify an experience, craft your story with purpose, and be deliberate about using the story to bring your message to life.

In the next chapter, we'll start to find out how.

Key Points

- Stories are our "native tongue," the way the brain naturally processes information. This makes storytelling familiar to us.

- Stories are a powerful means to engage an audience. They tap into neurochemicals and stimulate the brain. Oxytocin draws an audience in with reassurances of safety, cortisol grabs attention and grips them emotionally, and dopamine promises and delivers a reward. Together, they transport us from our here-and-now reality to join the storyteller inside the narrative.

- Well-told stories are engaging because they tap into our own memory storehouse of experiences. When we hear about situations and people we can relate to, they call up our own past experiences and mix into an intoxicating cognitive and emotional cocktail.

The best way to convey information so that it's understood and remembered is story. The best way to motivate action is story. Engaging stories are perhaps the most effective means we have to teach, lead, and inspire.

Application

1. Recall some memorable experiences from your life. What is it about them that makes them memorable? How many *facts* of do you recall vs. how many general *impressions* and *emotions* come to mind? This is the "secret" of the power of stories. (It's actually *science*, not secret.)

2. Next, look at other stories (movies, novels, news reports, etc.) and note how they, too, stimulate an emotional reaction in you when you watch/listen to them — even when they're fictional.

   What emotions do you experience?

   Which elements of the stories bring out these emotions?

   Do you notice similarities or patterns in the elements that consistently elicit similar emotions in you (e.g., plot twists, suspense, happy resolutions) If so, what are they?

3. Now, consider a message you want to convey to a person or group: a concept you want to teach, some behavior you want to influence, or someone you want to motivate or inspire.

   What story elements might help you achieve your goal, e.g., a vivid word picture, a memorable lesson learned, or a call to action?

Two: Use Stories to …

Now that we've discussed the power of stories and how they can be a useful tool to teach, lead, and inspire, let's consider how you can use them to support your business or personal objectives.

First, here are a few of the roles you might be in where stories can be effective to further your cause or reach your objectives:

Teacher and trainer — whether teaching school children, college students, or adult learners in a classroom or a corporate training room

Entrepreneur — pitching ideas, raising capital, getting employees on board, selling products, or talking to the media

Business leader — from the boardroom to the production line, and everywhere and everyone in between

Job searcher — whether looking to get a new position in an existing company or land a new opportunity

Parent/Grandparent — who are regularly in the role of teacher, leader, motivator, and advisor

You likely fit into at least one of those categories, and probably many of them. You may even think of additional roles you play where stories can help you teach, lead, and inspire. Great! The point is that stories carry power in any role you're in, and storytelling could be a useful tool to add to your skillset to help you achieve better results.

Now let's explore *how* you can use stories in these various roles. You'll notice that the categories of use cross over into many of the categories of users.

Stories to Teach

Think about the most impactful lessons you've learned and the people who taught those lessons. Go beyond your school years. Who were the corporate trainers, speakers, and church, business, or civic leaders you learned most from?

It's likely they were good storytellers. I hated most of my history classes because the "teachers" (they didn't teach me much) tried to fill my head with facts and figures. When I discovered that history is a collection of stories of those who were involved in significant acts, then history came alive and I learned much more than memorizing dates, locations, and names.

My friend Paul left a corporate job in marketing, got his teaching certificate, and started teaching middle school history. For any significant military conflict they are discussing, Paul dresses in the uniform of the soldiers to teach the lesson through stories of how the battles played out and the impact of those conflicts on the people. I'm betting his students remember their history lessons better than I remembered mine!

Whatever role you play, you'll likely find yourself teaching someone something. Instead of only throwing out facts and figures, teach with stories. The lessons will make more sense and will be remembered longer.

Stories to Sell

Most people try to convince or persuade someone by sharing facts and figures.

> "Our product runs twice as fast as the competition."

> "This car has 240 horsepower."

> "This shirt is 100 percent cotton."

Blah, blah, and blah.

If you want people to buy into your company, your product, or *you*, tell them stories that demonstrate how what you're offering connects to their needs. Stay out of the buzzword campaign, such as: "You'll be more productive, energetic, and attractive to all the hotties." Yuck! Instead, tell a story of how others have benefited or solved a problem with what you're offering.

Even if you don't have a sales position, you're likely selling at some point. Zig Ziglar said, "Maybe you don't hold the title of a salesperson, but if the business you are in requires you to deal with people, you, my friend, are in sales."

Even contract software developers who sit in front of a computer screen and pound out code have to talk to people at some point. Take Jeff, a software developer, who will have to sell himself to get the next job, sell why he used a particular methodology to a client, and maybe even persuade other programmers to cooperate with his ideas. Think of how much he will stand out from other contractors if he sells his idea with an impactful story.

If you're tempted with the thought, "But my data is soooooo compelling! I know this will win them over," then remember the experience we shared in the introduction to this book. The consultants had excellent survey data, but without the story of what that meant to company leaders, employees, and customers, clients weren't buying in. Go ahead and share your compelling data, then add a story that *shows* rather than *tells* how that information impacts the audience.

Stories to Climb the Ladder

Any time you're trying to get another job—whether a promotion in your company or a new position—you're selling yourself. Want to stand out from the other applicants? Don't answer questions with hackneyed lines that interviewers hear from every other candidate. Answer each question by sharing a short experience to illustrate your point.

What's the question you *hate* to get when you're in a job interview? If you're like most people, it's the dreaded, "What's your greatest weakness?" Now think about the last time you answered that question, or even about the advice you've been given as to how to answer that question. "Well, I'm too much of a perfectionist" or "My brilliance comes off as arrogance" or "I just care too deeply about other people." Does anyone really believe these answers?

What if, instead of giving one of those "suggested" answers, you shared an experience where you slipped up, made an honest mistake, and then recovered from that mistake and learned from it? That would show the interviewer an honest and humble side of you while still demonstrating positive character. More important, yours would be the answer the interviewer would remember.

For example, Alan worked for 10 years in marketing communications for a bank and decided he could reach his career goals more effectively by getting experience in another industry. He targeted high tech—a rather large leap from banking. He put together an impressive resume and portfolio and landed an interview with a software company.

After the opening pleasantries, the first question the interview asked was, "I see you've worked your entire career in banking. What makes you think you can be successful in high tech?" How's that for an opening salvo?!

Alan looked at the interviewer and responded, "Part of my last two jobs at the bank was taking complex information and making it understandable for people who were not as close to the topics. For example, I took information on a complex regulation and put it in terms that employees could understand and explain to their customers. I also helped introduce a new technology the bank was adopting by writing the letter that went to customers in language that was clear and non-technical. As a result, we exceeded our initial target for adoption of the technology. I think I could do the same for your company — take some of the complex technology and help people understand what it means to them."

The next week, Alan was offered the job.

When looking to advance in your company, don't just share the statistics on how long you've worked there, how many hours you've put in, or even the growth of a business line. Share a story about how you personally made a difference in fulfilling the mission of the organization and how that could be used in a higher position. Or tell about the time you helped a client solve a problem or reach an objective to show you could do more of that in a different role.

People remember stories. And hiring managers hire the people they remember. You'll sell yourself best with a powerful story.

Stories to Inspire

Sometimes what we ask of people is tough. It's hard work. It's not much fun. People start to wonder if it's worth the extra effort. This happens at home as well as at work. Try getting a teenager to clean the bathroom regularly and see if you get shouts of joy or grumbling complaints!

Yale psychologist Amy Wrzesniewski's research[1] shows that people have three different views of their work:

> 1) a *job* where they put in time and the only reward is a paycheck (these people typically do all they can to get away from work as fast as possible);

> 2) a *career* that includes the reward of advancement or achievement (in this case, the primary reason for doing the current job is to get the next one); or

> 3) a *calling* where they see work as rewarding in and of itself because of the contribution they are

making. These people give extra effort, often without being asked.

One of the interesting aspects of Wrzesniewski's research is that the work itself doesn't matter. Janitors can view their work as a calling while doctors can view their work as a job.

We sometimes try to motivate people with rah-rah speeches or by encouraging and praising their efforts: "Come on, you can do it!" Sincere praise is important, but a compelling story can help people see their work as more of a calling than a job, which increases motivation and output. Use stories to illustrate the value of what they are doing to help employees push through hard times—and they'll thank you for it.

A young company got a huge order at the beginning of December that they needed to fulfill before the first of the year. In order to meet that deadline, the employees would have to work extra hours during the year-end holiday season. How do you think that announcement went over? (Hint: Thud!)

Instead of telling employees, "Hey, this is what you get paid for. You should be happy to have a job," the leaders took the time to describe what the company could look like if they met this order. It was an "imagine when" type of story, painting a picture of company growth and success that would benefit each employee with fulfillment as well as financially.

Leaders acknowledged it would take extra effort and this was a busy time of year for employees personally. The company even offered benefits like shopping services to buy Christmas gifts and bringing in dinners on the nights that required extra work. Employees bought in, stepped up to the extra work, and the company—and each individual—realized the vision the leaders had painted in their story. It was fulfilling both personally and professionally for everyone.

Because stories are more memorable and emotionally connecting, they can get people through the tough times when success is just over the next hill.

Stories to Motivate Change

Many of the roles mentioned above—business leader, teacher, parent, etc.—require correcting people's behavior at some time. It's easy to say, "No, don't do it that way; do it this way." But people will be more motivated to change and will remember the correction more positively if they have context that a story can provide.

When receiving correction, people almost always want to know *why* they need to change, not just *what* they need to change. A simple story can make that difference, leading to less resistance and more probability that the change will stick.

For example, my friend Carrie worked as a volunteer in an office for a nonprofit organization. Volunteers were required to track the activity of patrons who used the facility. Volunteers came and went at different times throughout the week, and many of them took it upon themselves to change the process for tracking activity. The supervisor repeatedly told people, "You can't do it that way; you have to do it this way." People would change for a while then, when the supervisor wasn't around, would go back to a method they thought was easier.

Carrie asked the supervisor, "Why do we need to do it that way? What is it that makes this specific process better?" The supervisor explained that the paid staff had to review all the tracking forms at the end of each day, then compile and reconcile all the data. The approved process had a few more steps in it, but it made things easier for the staff at the end of the day. It also helped ensure accuracy between the different shifts.

When people started pushing back on the process, Carrie explained to them the benefits to the staff at day's end and the overall accuracy of reporting. She told of how one staff member had to stay late to reconcile the information because people weren't following the process. In addition, the inaccurate information made it harder to determine if they were serving their patrons as they wanted. Once people understood the ramifications of their actions, they were more willing to follow the approved process.

Tell a story that answers the *why* question to help not only correct the behavior, but to build more motivation to change their behavior for good.

Turn the Tables

Because you now understand the power of stories, you can help others tap into that power. Imagine this scenario. You're in a meeting where the head of customer service is sharing statistics about call volume and customer satisfaction scores. She's got a PowerPoint and everything. You know the kind: charts and graphs showing how this quarter's numbers compare with last quarter's numbers and the year-over-year comparison. Yawn. I feel myself slipping into a REM cycle just writing about it.

Turn the tables the same way *60 Minutes* creator Don Hewitt did as referenced in the previous chapter: "Tell me a story." Or more appropriately in this situation, say "Tell me *the* story." What's behind those numbers? Why is call volume up? Is there a problem with the product we need to fix? Is it user error that we can correct with a demo video on our support site? Do our customer service reps need additional training in explaining a recently identified problem? Or is the call volume a good indicator, pointing to increased sales and customer adoption? What's the story behind the change in call volume, either up or down? Without understanding the *why* behind the numbers, there's no way to replicate good trends or reverse negative trends.

James took a job in marketing for a tech company after several years in another industry. He wasn't a technologist, but a writer, and this company's products were high tech at its highest. In his second week, he was asked to write a white paper about a new product that was about to launch. He was sent to the technical product specialist — the person over all the development of the product — to get information for the release.

"Tell me about this new product," James started.

The product specialist went on and on about how great the technology was and how his software developers had written exceptional code that made them stand out from the competition. It was a bit like the proverbial asking a clockmaker what time it is. The description was a foreign language to James.

After a few minutes, James stopped the product manager and asked, "Who cares?"

The product manager was aghast. "Well, everyone cares! This is great stuff!"

"But who really cares about what your product does? And why do they care?" James was asking, "Tell me the story of what this product can do for customers?"

It was like pulling teeth to get beyond the technical details to the value the product delivered to the customer. Imagine how much more powerfully the message could have come across if the product manager had a great story to tell about a customer (or even a beta customer) who had experienced success with the product. What if the response to "tell me about the product" had been:

> The IT manager at a large manufacturing company was hesitant when we asked him to try our product. He'd heard promises of data security from vendors before and had been burned. They promised an easy recovery, but when the company experienced a power outage that unexpectedly fried one of their servers, it took two days to get all their data back. Even then, some of the recovered data had been corrupted and they lost customer records.
>
> So when we promised him immediate and accurate data recovery, you can imagine what he was thinking. The eye-rolling told us it was something like, "Here we go again!" Without our recovery guarantee and the simplicity of our interface, he likely wouldn't have given us a chance. We walked

him through the backup process. He was impressed by how easy it was but skeptical that we could deliver in a pinch.

Two weeks later, an employee accidentally introduced a virus into the company server, and the IT manager was dreading another painful data recovery process. He opened our software and clicked on the icon to recover data. What happened? The software restored all the company's data in less than 15 minutes! He took the next 30 minutes to verify that everything was intact and was thrilled to find how accurate the recovery was. That's what we're delivering with this product.

Be the one who says "Tell me a story!" when presented with only facts and figures. Not only will you benefit from the greater understanding, but your co-workers will thank you for helping them stay awake during those presentations!

Stories to Achieve ...

This is our catch-all category, and it's up to you to complete. Whatever you need or want to achieve when working with other people, stories can help get you there.

You could potentially use stories for challenges with family relationships, conflicts with neighbors or friends, to help in a tough job situation, or anything else. The point is to keep your mind open to opportunities where stories will be your most useful friend.

Whenever you find yourself stuck, you now know to ask yourself, "Is there a story that would help get me past this?" Anytime you need to make a point that is clear and memorable, use a story to help you.

No Manipulation Allowed

As you look for appropriate uses of stories to teach, lead, inspire, advance, motivate, etc., be careful that you don't use stories to accomplish unhealthy goals. If you try to use a story to manipulate, criticize, embarrass, or harass someone, it will backfire. Instead of leading to positive change and greater connection, your story will come across as condescending or attacking.

Also, don't use stories as an excuse for not having a direct conversation with someone when needed. Sometimes people will use stories to drop hints about an important issue that they'd prefer not to discuss directly, hoping that people will "get it" and change behavior. Sorry. A story alone likely won't help in that situation.

Let's say you're working on a cross-functional team and the person you rely on for information isn't following an established practice. This makes it harder for you to complete your part of the project because you have to rework some of the data you get from the co-worker. If you tell him a story about how following processes helped in another situation but don't mention the specific process you want him to follow, he may think that was a nice story that doesn't apply to him.

Stories can be helpful to illustrate the problem, but be sure to clearly identify the problem as well! This situation may not even require a story. More likely, this problem can be fixed by a simple conversation to find out why the person isn't using the established process and ask for a commitment to start using that process.

Stories can be powerful. But always use that power for good.

Key Points

Stories can be used for a variety of purposes. Our general categories of teach, lead, and inspire can be applied to many situations. Here are a few, but don't restrict your creative thinking to these:

- Stories to teach: Use stories to help make your teaching moments more memorable.

- Stories to sell: Instead of using buzzwords to sell your product, your company, or yourself, tell the story of the benefit you can provide. Show instead of tell!

- Stories to climb the ladder: Whether looking for a new job or to advance internally, share a story to demonstrate your value instead of using platitudes to describe your contributions.

- Stories to inspire: When you need people to step up, appeal to their highest selves with stories to demonstrate the purpose you're trying to achieve. Go beyond "rah-rah" speeches or coercion; stories will work better.

- Stories to motivate change: Help people understand *why* you want them to change with a story to illustrate the impact and you'll get less resistance.

- Turn the table: Get stories from other people. When they try to explain things in technical terms or with buzzwords, ask them to tell you a story that makes the point.

- Stories to achieve: You can use stories to achieve whatever you're trying to accomplish. If you look for options, you'll find ways to use stories that you might not have thought of before.

Finally, remember that the power of storytelling should never be used to manipulate or condemn people. Use the power of storytelling for good.

Application

1. Consider the different uses of stories described in this chapter: to teach, sell, climb the ladder, inspire, motivate change, and achieve in any number of ways.

   - In which of your roles could stories help the most? What benefit(s) are you trying to create or what problem(s) are you trying to resolve?

   - Who is the target audience for this story: one person? A few people? A large group?

   - What do you hope to accomplish with your story? Change their perspective? Improve their attitude or behavior? Motivate them to action?

2. To capture your ideas, you can take notes at the end of this and each subsequent chapter either in your own notebook or download our free Story Catcher at www.Master-Storytelling.com to guide you through this process.

Based on your answer, as you read the next chapter think of illustrations you could use that might move your audience in the way you hope.

Three: You Can Find Stories …

I was once chatting with a group of coworkers after a meeting. You've been in these kinds of conversations. The meeting wraps up, everyone gets up to go, someone asks a question like, "How was your weekend?" and you chat for a few minutes before getting back to work. It's great for team building and stress reduction.

I can't even remember the topic now, but it was lighthearted and I could relate to the subject. I chimed in with, "That reminds me of a time when . . ." I proceeded to tell a story connected to the topic. Everyone laughed. (Yes, it was funny!)

When the laughter died down, our intern, Josh, looked at me and said, "Do you have a story for everything?"

"What do you mean?" I responded. I really wasn't sure.

"It doesn't matter what topic comes up, you have a story about it," he said. "It's amazing."

The more I thought about his comment the more I realized that I pretty much do have a story for everything. That's because stories are *everywhere*. And if you're tuned into stories you can find stories that teach, lead, and inspire anywhere and everywhere.

As we were putting together our initial outline for this book, we probably took twice as long as we should have. Everything that came up reminded one of us (or both of us) of stories that related to the topic at hand. If you ever think, "I'm just not a storyteller," or "I can't think of any good stories," then this chapter will show you that you actually *do* have stories — loads of them. Your stories live in the day-to-day experiences you have, and even in experiences you hear from others. We'll help you tune into the experiences that are stories waiting to be told. The following chapters will then help you craft those experiences into stories you can use to illustrate, inspire, and instruct, even if you don't think you're a natural storyteller.

Humans are Story Machines

Stories are embedded into the brain processes of human beings. It's how we think. It's how we remember.

You're a storyteller whether you know it or not.

Don't believe us? Try this. Think about the last math or science class you had in high school. What are the first things that come to your mind? Quick—say them out loud or write them down.

Did your answers include the formulas you learned? Probably not. You likely recalled the room you were in, the teacher, the other students who sat around you, the experiments you ran, and if it was like my high school chemistry class, the smell of something burning from that last failed experiment. It was Chris' lab coat on fire or Kelly's pencil that shattered into thousands of pieces after it fell into the liquid oxygen.

What you remember are stories. You remember the *sense* you made of your experience: your surroundings, what happened there, and what it meant to you.

Sure, you may remember the facts and formulas (if you've continued to use them), but the most powerful memories and those that most readily come to mind are in the form of stories. Even when you draw the formulas and numbers out of the data-collecting portion of your brain, they likely didn't stir any emotion. But the sensory details—the sights, sounds, smells, faces, heat, cold, etc.—come from deep in your memory and put a smile on your face (or maybe a grimace) as the details come back to you.

Storytelling is your default setting. Sometimes you just need to be more deliberate in accessing that setting.

Finding Useful Stories

Once you are deliberate about noticing and collecting your stories, you'll start to see them everywhere. The key will be capturing them, putting them into a useful format, and practicing them to make them impactful. We'll give you more on the last two steps in later chapters. Let's talk first about capturing the stories that are all around you.

First, learn to recognize when an experience is impactful to you. Think about the past week. Mentally go through each day. What happened? What do you remember? What brings a smile to your face? What makes you cringe? What makes you angry? Which experiences did you tell other people about? Any of those situations could potentially be stories that can teach a principle or enhance an insight.

Anything that feels meaningful to you could be a story you can use at some point. It could be a time when you felt so frustrated that you stormed out of a room, then regretted it later. Or maybe a time when you couldn't stop laughing because the experience was so funny, and you couldn't wait to tell someone about it. The experiences don't have to be grand and glorious; even simple experiences can teach a point. It could be a time when you thought, "I wonder why that happened?" or "This doesn't make any sense at all!" It could be a moment of minor irritation or something that made you smile (as opposed to laugh out loud).

Pay attention to those moments when your internal voice tells you something is good, bad, great, terrible, emotionally stirring, important, informative, interesting, odd, etc. Any "ah-ha" that hits you means you've come across something you could use as a story. You'll find them everywhere if you look for them regularly.

When the emotion strikes, take a note. As you're building your storytelling capacity, a mental note won't be good enough. Write it down. Keep a notebook close to you (if you're old school) or store the experience in your electronic device (we know you'll have that close). A quick voice memo to yourself will even suffice. You don't have to write out or explain the whole experience, just capture enough of it to make sure you can recall the details later. Be sure to record why you thought it was meaningful or impactful in the moment.

For example, recently I was traveling to speak at a leadership conference for a company. I gave the same presentation to a similar group at this company a few months earlier. The event was at the same hotel where they had made a reservation for me the last time we had this event. I got to the hotel about 9:30 p.m. only to learn there was no reservation for me — and the hotel had no availability. I hadn't checked to see if the client was going to make a reservation for me as they had before and, apparently, they didn't. Fortunately, I travel enough that I have pretty good status with Marriott, so I called the customer service number and they found me a hotel only a half mile away. Whew.

I'm not sure yet how I'm going to use that story, but I will eventually. I could use it to talk about the danger in making assumptions. I could also use it to demonstrate the power of good service from Marriott. Or I could use it to illustrate flexibility. I'm not sure yet. But when it happened, it was meaningful to me, so I'm keeping it in my story bank for future reference.

Watch. Listen. Observe.

Another approach you can take is to think about what points you frequently need to illustrate. Whether you're using your stories to teach a course, inspire a team, make a sale, or get a promotion, think about the topics that you may need to showcase through a story. Write down a few of those topics and look at the list every day. You may be surprised at how many things happen that you'll be able to notice and capture because you were paying attention. As the American sage Yogi Berra pointed out, "You can observe a lot by just watching!"

Here are a few areas of your life where you can watch, listen, and observe to capture stories:

Your own experiences. These are the best stories to tell because you're closest to them and you understand the impact best. You'll be able to describe the emotion from a first-person perspective. Again, pay attention to what is meaningful or impactful to you on any given day. You may not know what to do with the experience immediately but, at some point, that will be a story you can use.

Other people's experiences. Listen to other people sharing what has happened to them, even in casual conversation, and you'll find stories that make the points you want to make. Recently, my sister shared an experience she had trying to pay a bill. She went through three different people in the "customer service" department at the company who all cited "policy" as a reason for not being able to help her. The irony is she was trying to make a payment, and the company wouldn't accept the payment because of "policy." I used her example two weeks later to illustrate how a lack of flexibility creates a culture where policy comes before people to the detriment of the company.

You don't have to be sneaky about using the experiences of others. When you find yourself looking for an experience to illustrate a topic, ask others if they've had an experience or know of an example.

My friend Dennis was looking for an illustration about groups that failed to collaborate simply because they weren't thinking from the perspective of other people.

He was stumped. All the examples he could come up with seemed to show that people were being selfish, but he wanted an example that showed that sometimes people act in unhelpful ways innocently, without realizing they are doing anything wrong. He mentioned his conundrum to his wife, who said, "I've got a perfect example." The story was about a husband who came home with a gift for his wife, who was eight months pregnant. The gift? An ab roller! He thought he was being nice; the pregnant wife felt otherwise!

News and current events. Pay attention to the world around you and you'll find illustrations of almost any point you want to make. Granted, most of the news coverage is negative, and you'll have to stay away from potentially distracting topics (race, religion, politics, etc.), but there's a lot of potential in current events.

For example, a freeway overpass in the Atlanta area caught fire from some flammable materials left beneath the bridge. As a result, traffic was impacted for months in the metropolitan area. You could use this story to illustrate the ripple effects of one seemingly insignificant act on many other people. We keep repeating this, but it bears repeating: Look at current events and news stories in the context of the point you're trying to make and you'll likely find lots of examples.

History. People can relate to historical events and figures. Use their stories as illustrations of the lessons you want to teach. Looking for an example of leadership? Look to history for people who led a nation or an army to victory against the odds. Maybe you need to reinforce teamwork. Which sports teams or companies rallied together with fewer assets than their competitors and came out on top? The world has been around for a long time. Any topic you want to teach has probably already been illustrated by someone else's example.

Our caution here is to make sure the stories are actually true and not urban legends. If you present a story as historical that is actually not true, you run the risk of your listeners thinking, "Yeah, but that never really happened," and invalidating your point.

For example, for years children in the United States were repeatedly told the story of the first U.S. president, George Washington, cutting down his father's cherry tree as a boy. His admission of guilt was a lesson on the power of honesty. The problem is no one can source George Washington ever relating that experience, and there are no indications that there was ever a cherry tree on the property where young George grew up. Use historical events, but make sure they're really historical. Part of the irony in this example is that for years people told a story that wasn't true to illustrate the importance of being honest. Hmmm.

Literature, television, and movies. Sometimes it's easy to let the professional storytellers tell the story for you. You've likely seen inspiring movies or television clips that bring a point home. You can retell those stories (or with the right permission even show the clip) to make important points. One of my favorite illustrations is the plot of the movie *Groundhog Day*, where Bill Murray's character, Phil Connors, lives the same day over and over again until he finally changes from being selfish to helpful. At first, he did the same thing every day, expecting that somehow the outcome would change. Sometimes, we do the same thing in our lives: we keep trying the same tactics over and over and hope things will get better. Until we try something different, our results likely won't change.

Two cautions around literature and pop culture. First, if you're using literature, television, or film to tell a vision story—about how your team or organization can overcome odds to get to a bright future, for example—make sure you pull from real life events, not fiction. Draw on movies and books about the lives of real people and real events. The fictional accomplishments will fall flat as an inspiration to get people to strive to attain real accomplishments because they're made up. It's easy for people to think, "Sure that works in fantasy land, but it can't work here."

Second, make sure your audience is familiar with the content you're drawing from. I was giving a presentation that included the *Groundhog Day* illustration I mentioned previously to a group of people from Tanzania and Kenya. As I got to that point in the presentation, I realized it would fall flat, so I skipped it. They don't have groundhogs in Africa, much less a holiday named for the rodent. And while the movie has broad appeal in the United States, it wasn't a hit in Africa.

We hope these ideas have spurred some stories in you already. If not, don't worry. Look around — you'll find them. Stories are everywhere, and your stories are just waiting to be told.

Key Points

- Stories are all around you! Any experience that seems meaningful, impactful, emotional, etc. could be turned into a story. Watch for those experiences and take note when they happen, even if you don't yet know how you'll turn the experience into a story.

- When you have a concept or principle you need to teach, look for experiences that could illustrate your point. If you can't find any in your own life, ask friends and family members if they know of an experience that would make your point.

- You can also borrow stories from literature, history, movies (particularly history-based), and from the experiences of others. Don't limit yourself on where you find stories to teach, lead, and inspire. They're everywhere!

Application

Now it's time to apply what you've just learned.

1. Identify two to four points you regularly need to make with audiences (clients, teams, etc.), especially those you identified in the Application section of chapter 2. These could be subjects like teamwork, innovation, focus, continuous improvement, etc. Write all these topics down somewhere and then review them **every morning for two weeks**.

2. During those two weeks, keep a journal of potential stories that come from your own personal experiences, the experiences of others, current events, history, or the media. You don't need to write out the entire story, just some of the key points: who was involved, what happened, where it took place, the impact, the emotion, etc. Look for moments that were meaningful to you; that's your trigger. Look

particularly for experiences that illustrate the points you identified in step 1.

At the end of two weeks, identify one experience to use in an upcoming presentation, class, or meeting. You don't need to specify the exact date or time, but which experience could potentially illustrate one of your key points. You'll also use that experience in subsequent activities at the end of upcoming chapters.

Four: Great Stories Include …

Three-year-old Eli was starting to become more social, just as he was learning to string together coherent sentences. Eli has an engaging smile that leads strangers to strike up conversations with him.

The only problem is that Eli has a limited vocabulary. So sometimes Eli can't continue conversations very well after they get started.

"What's your name?"

"Eli."

"How old are you?"

Holding up three fingers while exerting great effort to keep the other fingers on that hand down. "Three."

"What do you like to do?"

Blank stare.

At this point, Eli resorts to what he knows. He points to his baby brother in the stroller next to him. "That's Curtis. He's my brother."

Never mind that this response has nothing to do with the question that was asked. Eli knows *this* answer, so he goes to it when he's not sure what else to say.

We can cut Eli some slack—after all, he's only three. But adults do this too. It's a natural reaction. Anyone who has learned a second language can probably recall a time when they were talking to a native speaker of that language and heard vocabulary they didn't know. What did they do? Go back to the words and phrases they're familiar with, even if they don't completely fit with the conversation. Maybe try to bluff their way through with some simple phrases they do know.

When it comes to teaching and leading, storytelling might not be your native language. You may find it easier to go back to simply telling people what to do or illustrating your points with data, charts, graphics, and your impressive knowledge of the topic. But once you learn the language of storytelling—the structure, the uses, questions to ask—you'll feel more comfortable using this new language to teach, lead, and inspire.

You've likely experienced a time when a story has fallen flat. You may have heard the old joke about a man who was convicted of a crime and sentenced to prison. During lunch on his first day behind bars, another inmate stood up and shouted, "Twenty-one!" Everyone in the room laughed. After a while, another person yelled, "This is a classic: thirty-six." Everyone roared. After a couple more minutes someone shouted, "Fifty-five," and the room erupted in laughter again.

The new inmate turned to the guy next to him and asked, "What's that all about?"

"Oh," the seasoned inmate explained, "we've all been in here so long that we've memorized the jokes everyone tells. Now we don't even have to tell the joke. We just say the number, and everyone knows why it's funny."

Wanting to ingratiate himself to his new community, the inexperienced inmate thought he'd give it a try. He stood up and yelled, "Eighteen." No one laughed. A few inmates looked at him in disdain while others groaned and rolled their eyes.

Embarrassed, the new inmate sat down and whispered to his neighbor, "That was a disaster! What happened?"

The inmate took another bite of mashed potatoes, looked at his new friend, and said, "Well, some people just don't know how to tell a good joke."

Crafting a Good Story

Sometimes we think a story is funny or impactful, but everyone listening only chuckles awkwardly or looks confused. It seems some people just don't know how to tell a good story.

If you've ever put yourself in that category—or if you've ever told a story that didn't have the impact you hoped—we'll provide ways in this chapter to help you out. Even if you're an experienced storyteller, we think you'll find these tips will help you more consistently deliver a story that fulfills your goals. We'll also show you how structuring your story appropriately helps stir up the biological triumvirate of oxytocin, cortisol, and dopamine in your audience that we talked about in chapter one.

This chapter will *not* give you a strict storytelling script to follow. There are a number of ways to tell a good story. Forcing yourself into a specific script will make your story sound, well, scripted. Then you risk it losing impact. Tell the story as you would tell it to a friend, with authenticity.

On the other hand, great storytelling goes beyond relating your experience as it happened. If you want your experience to teach, lead, and inspire, you'll need to structure the experience into a story so that it has maximum impact. As you do so, keep these points in mind.

Audience First

I recently heard a nurse relate an experience about two patients she was working with. Her point was to show how people handle adversity in different ways, for an audience of people from a variety of backgrounds—

very few of whom worked in the healthcare industry. Several times she threw out medical terms as though everyone would know what she meant. The illustration was good, but the frequent reference to medical terminology was distracting for me. "She had a PUD so was in quite a bit of pain." A *what*? "Another patient was experiencing dysphagia." *Dis-huh?* I found myself thinking so hard about what the terms might mean—or asking my wife who does understand medical terms— that I missed some key points of the story.

Consider your audience when crafting and telling your story. Who are you talking to? What do they know? What do they *not* know? What level and kind of vocabulary do they use? What examples or illustrations will they understand?

Everyone has had adversity, even if it was a minor illness. You don't have to be a medical professional to understand pain or discomfort. But you should tell the story differently to a group of lay people than to medical professionals.

Relatable Characters, Real Emotions

Characters are the essence of a good story. Think about the last time you watched a movie and then walked away from it feeling disappointed. You may have been interested in the plot but for some reason the movie didn't satisfy you. The reason is likely because you couldn't relate to the characters.

So, begin your story by introducing likable, relatable characters who are set in a familiar context and who face situations similar to what the audience has faced. This will stimulate oxytocin in your listeners. Oxytocin builds trust and reassures them. It helps them feel safe, open, willing, and persuades them to take the journey with you. Relatable characters draw people into your story; they'll want to be part of what you're sharing.

Ask yourself, who are the main people in the story that your audience needs to relate to and understand how they feel? What is it about those characters that they can relate to? What are the emotions that will help people connect to the main point of your story? Keep those questions in mind as you establish the characters in your story.

But this can be a challenge. What if you have a mixed audience with a wide variety of backgrounds and education levels? Many organizations have multiple generations of workers. Those generations carry different perspectives on life. You may even have audiences with wide-ranging cultural backgrounds.

People relate to other people who are like them in some way. As you develop your stories, describe the characters in a way that your audience can connect with. Some things are universal: We've all felt nervous or anxious or happy or excited or embarrassed. Bring out the emotions that are common to the human experience. Look for common ground. You'll likely be able to find areas they all can relate to. Remember, the one thing every person on this earth has in common is that each of us is human! Many of your stories likely connect to the human condition: love, fear, ambition, belonging, etc. But if you must use terms or examples that some people may not understand, give a quick explanation so that everyone can follow your story. If you really need to use *dysphagia*, simply explain that it means difficulty swallowing.

When relating your personal experiences, you may feel a bit nervous about expressing the depth of emotions you were feeling. But the more honest you are with your emotions (even if they're negative) the more people will relate to the story and to you as the teller. As famed psychologist Carl Rogers said, "What is most personal is most universal."

If you aren't authentic in telling your own stories, the audience will sense it. We're not suggesting you have to jump up and down with excitement like a high school cheerleader or bring yourself to tears like an Olympian saluting the flag on the medal stand. Simply be honest about the emotions of the moment (like the cheerleader and Olympic champion are) and your audience will connect better with the story. Authenticity will breed credibility, which is another way to increase oxytocin in your listeners.

Much of the trust you build by sharing your personal experiences will come from being vulnerable. If you trust your listeners enough to share your experiences — even those when you stumbled along the way — they will return that trust to you. Trust begets trust and, as a result, oxytocin increases.

Of course, you want to avoid the deadly polar opposites of bragging on the one hand and being a miserable failure on the other. When we brag, it discourages others from liking and rooting for us. Instead, they will tend to oppose us, hoping we fall on our face and get our just deserts.

On the other hand, while being a failure may make people root for you, they won't last long in a losing effort. They want to hear a story of hope, of ultimate triumph, and see an example of how they, too, can overcome their challenges and win in the end. So, if you're going to tell a cautionary tale — a time when things didn't work out for you — turn it into a teaching moment when you gained insight into what you *should* have done: the skill you should have used, the action you should have taken, the time when you should have (for example) shut your mouth.

Problems and Resolutions

A story without problems is about as interesting as someone else's family reunion video. ("Oh, and there's Uncle Billy, and my other Uncle Willy.") It doesn't produce the cortisol to keep us alert and interested. There needs to be some kind of conflict and resolution in your story to keep the audience's attention and get your point across. If there's no problem, there's no point. We like what Judy Garland said: "I try to bring the audience's own drama—tears and laughter they know about—to them." If you can bring to your audience the drama they can relate to, you'll have them hooked into your story.

The conflict in your experience stimulates a cortisol kick. You can introduce risk, surprise, conflict, and even danger into your story. You can build suspense, make the next step or outcome mysterious (keep 'em guessing), or introduce a twist in the plot to keep listeners on the edge of their seats (literally or figuratively). These all heighten listeners' senses and put their brains on high alert about what may harm the characters in the story they care about, or that the outcome may be different from what they expect.

Drama doesn't have to be breathtaking and theatrical. It can be as simple as feeling embarrassed because you messed up an assignment or showed up at the wrong time for a meeting. Drama can be as common as racing hard to meet an important deadline and feeling a sense of accomplishment when you get it done on time. Remember, stories are about sense-making. Stories illustrate a point or principle by dressing it up in real life. They add color and clarity to abstractions.

The reason that risk, conflict, and danger get—and hold—our attention is because they pose a potential loss, and we humans *hate* to lose something we value. In fact, research shows that we're more motivated to avoid losing something we value than we are driven to attain the very same thing. This *loss aversion* promotes feelings of vigilance, including increasing our heart rate, sharpening our focus, and putting us at the ready to respond to whatever threatens to take away the thing we value. This includes tangible items (like money or health) and intangible possessions (our reputation, status, sense of self-worth).

We can pique loss aversion in a story by introducing an emotional threat. I goofed up in public. My ego was on the line. I had to eat crow for something I said. I made a career-limiting move at work. These tap into one of the most common fears adults have—the fear of looking stupid. Once you connect an audience to one of their own fears, you've got them hooked.

Resolutions can be both successes and stumbles. Particularly when telling a story about ourselves, we like to share the times we succeeded and hide the times we failed. But failure stories sometimes have just as much impact when used as cautionary tales, especially if you're helping a group bounce back from a disappointment.

Years ago — which is to say "back when I was young and stupid" — I was traveling on business. After a long day, I got to my hotel room and opened my email. One message was from a co-worker in another department in our division, questioning the approach my team was taking on a project. He sent the message to me, but also copied my boss.

I rolled my eyes. Who was he to criticize? He clearly didn't have all the facts and wasn't even smart enough to get the facts right that he did have.

In my tired and annoyed state, I whipped off an email to my boss. Since she had been copied on the original message, I felt the need to let her know that I was going to talk to the co-worker about this issue. I also took the opportunity to make sure she knew how idiotic I thought this co-worker's opinions were. I may have used some dismissive phrase like, "I'll talk to him and let him know how clueless he is."

The next morning, to my horror, I opened my email to find that instead of sending my message as a "forward" to my boss, I had hit "reply" and the message went to the coworker — including my snippy and sarcastic comments about his intelligence and inability to process simple information.

Can you feel the pit in your stomach that I felt in that moment? I was sick. My message was immature, inconsiderate, and just plain stupid. Even sending that message to my boss was the wrong decision.

To my coworker's credit, he responded to the email with, "I think you meant to send this to Cheryl, not me. But I look forward to talking with you about it when you get back to the office." We did have the conversation, but I had to own up to some seriously bad judgement as part of the discussion.

I'm confident that you sensed how this was going to turn out by about the second paragraph. So, why did you read it to the end? It wasn't just to finish the task of reading; it was because you started releasing cortisol as you saw my story going sideways. You anticipated the social danger I was in and pretty much knew I was going to embarrass myself with my coworker, and maybe my boss. And you were right! But even though you knew more or less how the story would go, you felt compelled to read the rest of it to see how this train wreck actually went off the rails. That's cortisol's clout.

Finally, we can give our audience a tasty hit of dopamine when we give them a pay-off — a satisfactory ending to our story or a bit of humor along the way. These satisfactory endings are often *happy* endings where the character overcame challenges or succeeded against odds. (Whew!) But they can also be cautionary tales, showing how mistakes led to an unfavorable outcome that we can learn from for "next time." The story about my email exchange above is an example of the latter. Both can stimulate dopamine because of the relief at the end. Dopamine makes us feel more optimistic, positive, and hopeful—a great way to leave people feeling at the end of your story.

But don't assume people will automatically see the conflict and resolution. Ask some questions to get them engaged. (More on that in the next chapter.) Make obvious the stress the character(s) felt and what important objective they may or may not achieve. Without some potential problem, the story isn't interesting or engaging. And with no resolution, you leave people hanging, aching to make sense of the struggle. Without that resolution, they don't get that exhilarating hit of dopamine that makes stories so rewarding.

Direct Dialogue

To make the point of this next section, I want to give you two contrasting examples from a story I've told before. The examples pick up in the middle of the story to make a point, so don't get distracted by not getting the entire story here. (You can read the complete story in the Appendix at the end of the book under the title "Ethical Emergency.") Read through the two examples that follow and think about the differences between them.

Example 1

After reading the paragraph, Ed (the CTO) wanted to know why I added it. I explained that Chad (the CEO) wanted it to be included.

Ed shook his head and told me that the feature wasn't even in this version of the product. In fact, he said they were hoping to have that feature ready for the next version, but he wasn't sure if they could make it work.

I figured Chad must have misunderstood, so I went back to him and shared what I learned from Ed. I told Chad that, based on this new information, I was going to take that information out of the press release.

Chad's response was that he knew it wasn't in this version, but he wanted me to leave the paragraph in and make it defensible. I wasn't even sure what that meant, so I asked him. He wanted me to write the information in a way that we could explain that we really meant it was in the next version of the product — even though we knew that wasn't true. His motivation was that this feature made us look better than the competition.

I didn't think that was a good idea, and I told Chad that I disagreed. He basically told me to do what he said because he signs the paychecks. Then told me to get out of his office.

Example 2

After reading the paragraph, Ed (the CTO) said, "Why did you add this paragraph?"

"Chad (the CEO) said it needed to be included," I replied.

Ed shook his head. "Nope. That feature isn't in this version of the product. We're hoping to develop it for the next version, but we're not even 100 percent sure we can do it."

I figured Chad must have misunderstood, so I went back to him and said, "Ed tells me that feature isn't in this version of the product, so I'm going to take that paragraph out of the press release."

Chad responded, "I know it's not in this version, but leave the paragraph in. Just make it sound defensible."

Defensible? I wasn't even sure what he meant by that, so I asked.

He explained, "Write it in a way that if anyone asks us about it we can say we really meant it was going to be in the next version. This is a really important feature that will make us stand out from the competition. It needs to be in there."

I said, "I don't think that's a good idea. That could really come back to haunt us." I was trying to protect the company and him ... and myself! I would be the one who had to "defend" the statement.

Chad's eyes narrowed and his voice raised. "Look," he said, "you work for me. I sign the paychecks. You do what I tell you to do. Now get out."

The Difference?

What do you see as the major difference between those two examples? And what difference does that make to the hearer of the story?

The difference is dialogue. Actual words that were spoken instead of summaries of what was spoken. Many storytellers—especially when first learning the skill—*describe* what happened in the experience, but don't include actual dialogue between the characters in the story. Dialogue makes a difference. A big difference.

As you read the two examples of the same experience above, you probably felt differently while reading the second version than the first. Dialogue draws you into the story, making you feel as though you are a witness to the conversation. Dialogue helps you understand the characters, conveys the conflict, elevates emotions, and leads to resolution (or the lack thereof). As a result, you feel more emotions when you hear the actual dialogue, which triggers the positive benefits of brain chemistry.

In addition, dialogue is often more succinct, which will keep your story moving forward. Dialogue is efficient, a quick back-and-forth to transfer meaning. Descriptions of dialogue are slower and harder to follow. Take advantage of the way humans naturally communicate by using specific dialogue in your stories.

Make the Point Clear

Almost everyone has seen this mistake. A presenter tells a funny story to start a speech. The audience laughs, and he moves on. Then you sit and wonder, "What was that all about?"

Don't leave your audience in doubt of the point you are trying to make. Part of the challenge here is that many stories can make many different points. That's the power of stories. If you want your audience to remember a certain principle, thought, or lesson, make that connection for them as you wrap up your story. If you don't, they'll make their own connections, and they may not be the connections you want them to make.

As you develop the conflict and resolution of your story, keep the ending in mind. Where are you heading? This will help you include the important details and leave out the extraneous fluff. As best-selling author Malcolm Gladwell says:

One of the mistakes I think writers make is they spend a lot of time thinking about how to start their stories and not a lot of time thinking about how to end them. Knowing my ending makes the beginning super easy. It's totally clear what I have to do and totally clear what I shouldn't do.[1]

Here's a place you'll have to practice some balance. While you want to make your point clear, you don't necessarily want to end with an explicit, "And the moral of this story is …" Structure your story so the resolution (or lack of resolution) of the conflict demonstrates the concept you're communicating. Whatever comes after your story can help make that connection as well. For example, you might share a story with your team about how someone stepped up to make sure an important project was successful. The next item on your agenda may be the upcoming project that will require the same type of effort from your team. Conversely, another way to ensure that the point of your story is clear is to introduce your main idea up front and then use the story to illustrate it.

If your story is designed to teach a concept or principle, you can use questions to assess the learning point. We'll go on a deeper journey into questions in the next chapter, but consider how a simple assessment at the end of your story could be powerful. As you conclude your experience, you might ask "What helped this go well?" Or in the case of a mistake story,

"What could I have done differently?" Even if your audience doesn't give the exact answer you expect, this gives you a chance to guide them to the point you want to make with your story.

When telling a story to move someone to action—to make a change, to step up to a challenge, etc.—end with a simple *call to action*. This is another place where a question could be useful. Ask your team if they're ready to step up to the challenge, if they'll follow the new process, whatever you're asking them to do. You may also need to assess whether they have questions about next steps. Your story may have been powerful enough to motivate change, but if they don't know *what* to do, the change is unlikely.

There is great power in choice. By ending with an invitation to act, you give people a chance to say "yes"—and if you've told your story well, they likely will be ready to act. The simple act of verbalizing their commitment creates a personal motivation to follow through. Give a powerful boost to the motivation that comes from your story by giving an invitation that allows people to choose to act.

A Little Humor Never Hurts

Yet another way to stimulate dopamine is to make people laugh. We trust people who can tickle our funny bone. It's the sweetener to the tale. When you can tell an interesting story *and be funny along the way*, listeners stick with you to the end.

This is why we love stand-up comedians so much. They tell relatable stories in a humorous way. Herbert Gardner pointed out the power of humor: "Once you get people laughing, they're listening, and you can tell them almost anything." (Use that power ethically, of course.)

Two points on humor. First, if it's not a natural language to you, don't force it. As with most skills, humor can be learned. But if it's awkward or uncomfortable for you, don't feel obligated to try to be funny.

Second, use humor appropriately. If you're sharing an experience to make a serious point, humor might be distracting. Also, stay away from sensitive topics such as politics, religion, nationality, etc. Your story isn't a place to use edgy humor that you might get away with among close friends. Humor can also be distracting if it's overused. If you spend so much time in your story trying to be funny, listeners may miss the point. Sure, they'll be full of dopamine, but you'll miss your goal of teaching, leading, and inspiring. And all the dopamine in the world can't make up for that loss.

How Much?

One of the many challenges of storytelling is to know which details to include and which to leave out. As you're creating relatable characters, demonstrating how they're feeling, walking the audience through the problem and resolution, and ensuring you're making the point, it's easy to start rambling. Or when it's your own experience, you can recall so many vivid details that your listeners will get lost in the minutia and miss the point. On the other hand, you may gloss over details that your audience needs to make sense of the situation. *You* know what happened and can see it clearly in your mind, but they don't have the rich background you have by having lived the experience.

Again, we don't want to set hard-and-fast rules on the length of a story, but a good rule of thumb is about **two to three minutes**. Include the necessary information so the story makes sense and makes the point, and that's all. Keep the story long enough to cover the subject, but short enough to remain interesting.

The Multi-Story

If you have a longer, more complex story that makes multiple points, consider sharing it in portions. Give the introduction to the story, then come back and finish it later. I sometimes share an experience my son had in high school about a miscommunication with a teacher. The first point in the story is about trying to solve the wrong problem. Another point the story illustrates is how to correct those mistakes when they happen. I tell the first part of the story, then teach the skill for handling the problem. Then I go back to the story later to illustrate how those skills work. This is a good strategy to build suspense, keep focused when there is more than one point, and it doesn't choke your audience by feeding them too much all at once.

One caution on this approach: Don't forget to go back to the end of the story or you'll leave people hanging! I did that once and, after the presentation, someone approached me and said, "So, how does that story end?" I realized I'd left everyone else dangling, wondering the same thing. In addition to missing a valuable teaching opportunity, the audience failed to get the dopamine satisfaction from the story's conclusion.

Key Points

When putting your story together, remember:

- Keep your audience in mind. Use language and examples they can understand and that connect to their lives.

- Develop relatable characters. People relate best to people who are like them in some way. What are the characters thinking? What are they feeling? Use common examples.

- Clarify the conflict or problem. What's getting in the way of success? What's at risk?

- Use dialogue. Share the specifics of any conversations that took place during the experience to bring life to the story.

- Make the point. Be sure you're clear on what you want people to take away from the story and be sure the audience is clear on your point.

- Be succinct. Keep your story within about two to three minutes. If you have a longer story, look for opportunities to break it into smaller parts and share a multi-part story.

Application

Take the experience you identified in the last chapter and outline it with the following points:

1. Think about your audience. What can they relate to in this story? Is there terminology you need to use (or stay away from) for this particular audience?

2. Who are the characters the audience will relate to? What emotions are they likely feeling? How can you express those concisely yet vividly to the audience?

3. What conflict is the main character facing? What are the potential problems in not resolving that conflict? What are the benefits of resolving the conflict?

4. How does your story get to a resolution — either success or a lesson learned?

5. How clear is the point you're making? How can you illustrate the main principle while leaving room for your audience to draw their own lessons from it as well?

You may outline the story a couple of different ways for different audiences. Think through how the story might be altered for different audiences you address.

Five: How Can Questions Help?

Oh my soul, be prepared for the coming of the Stranger.
Be prepared for him who knows how to ask questions.

~ T. S. Eliot

The obvious role of a storyteller is to *tell* a story. But storytelling to teach, lead, and inspire is not just about conveying information, or even being entertaining. To be successful as a purposeful storyteller, we must engage our listeners' minds and hearts: help them understand what we're saying and really feel it. As we just covered in the previous chapter, we can do that through vivid word crafting, introducing them to interesting characters, developing intriguing plot lines with surprising twists, and then giving them a nice reward at the end for having taken the journey with us. To this list, let's add a typically overlooked tool: *questions*. Well-crafted questions are a means to hook our listeners' minds and insert them into our narrative so that they can *feel* it.

Let's try out the power of questions right now. What is the predominant color of the clothes in your closet?

Whether you can answer that question accurately or not, there's one thing we know about your brain: It's thinking about the color of the clothes in your closet. It can't help it. Questions hijack your mental processes and demand center stage, and you can't stop them. In fact, research[1] has shown that just asking someone about their intention to complete a future task (e.g., voting, donating blood, exercising) increases the likelihood that they'll actually do it. That's power!

As you've been reading this book, you've probably been paying more attention to some things we've been saying and focusing less on others. Some parts probably struck a chord with you and other parts may have barely stirred your consciousness. (That's also how people will listen to your stories.) But when I posed that question about your clothes, your brain perked up and rushed to respond. That's what brains do. In fact, as you've read this paragraph, your mind is probably still trying to figure out which color dominates your closet. Why is that? (Oops, another question!)

Physiologically, your brain can focus on only one thing at a time; this is why, for example, distracted driving is a real problem.[2] So, when you're asked a great question, your brain is like a detective: It's on the case! The question burrows its way into your consciousness and won't let you rest until you've solved the mystery. Questions create curiosity.

Often, when you pose a question, a gap is created between what you know and what you want to know. This void grabs your attention and won't let go until it's satisfied, the mystery solved. At other times, questions cover areas you already know, but that's okay, too. They're a powerful way to focus your audience. In fact, that's exactly why we've sprinkled questions throughout the book—to focus your brain on a specific point we're trying to make.

You've already experienced this power of questions, probably many times (not counting the color-of-your-closet-clothes question). Perhaps you've been talking to a friend about some topic and, in the course of the conversation, you suddenly recall something oh so vaguely—the kid in third grade who had a similar experience, or the coworker who shared a quote related to it, or the radio news program where some expert discovered the secret that relates to your current conversation. That absent fact, the memory ghost that just eludes your grasp, takes center stage in your mind and insists on being recalled. Such is the power of a question, be it, "What was that kid's name?" or "What was that new discovery you recently heard about?" The question grabs you and won't let go.

This is a power that we, as storytellers, can use to good effect. Well-*formed* questions stimulate audience members' brains and get them thinking about what you're telling them. Well-*placed* questions can carry listeners along your narrative path.

The Power of Great Questions

We can tap the power of questions to enliven our stories in a number of ways. First, sprinkling in a well-placed question breaks up our story into "bite-sized" chunks that make it easier to digest. When you ask a question, you make your listeners pause and "chew on" what you've told them to that point. As with food, this starts the digestion process, as well as allowing your listeners to savor the flavor of your narrative. Questions have this duel benefit—they help listeners enjoy the story more, but also remember the point more fully.

A well-formed question actively draws your audience into the story. As listeners, they're in a passive mental state, metaphorically sitting on the back seat of a tandem bike—and you're doing all the pedaling. Ask them a question and they switch to active participants: They start pedaling with you. They go from passively listening to your narrative to actively participating in your experience. They get more engrossed in the story as they actively travel the narrative path alongside you.

Questions also enhance your story by drawing out listeners' own stories. One reason we experience connection to a well-told story is because we've lived something similar ourselves. Questions take us back to our own experiences and invite us to apply them to the story we're now listening to. This *déjà vu* dynamic creates an urge to join the story that's as irresistible as it is automatic.

When listeners pause to consider a question, search for an answer, then find it, they *feel* the story more. Good questions are another way to unleash the power of oxytocin, cortisol, and dopamine, all in one fell swoop.

Crafting Great Questions in Storytelling

So, what kinds of questions give us this boost in our stories? Since oxytocin causes us to empathetically relate to others, allowing us to walk in another person's shoes for a time, the kinds of questions that can release it in our listeners include:

> *Have you ever felt that way?*
>
> *Can't you just sense how (happy, disappointed, elated, shocked) Morgan was?*
>
> *As a parent (classmate, coworker, etc.), when have you faced a similar situation?*
>
> *How might you feel if this were happening to you?*

Cortisol is an agitator. Its release increases attention, and it begins to flow when we ask questions like:

> *What do you think happened next?*

Would you believe (plot twist) happened?

Think about what was on the line.

(Note that this is an implied question. You don't always have to end a question with a question mark.)

Questions activate dopamine by promising an answer—if only the listener can find it. The activity of searching for, and then finding, an answer pays a nice reward. Ahhhhh! Examples of questions that stimulate a dopamine release include:

In your opinion, what made the difference? What was the key to resolving this?

What's your take-away from this experience? What's a lesson-learned?

How glad do you think I was that I used that skill and solved the problem?

A Framework for Creating Good Questions

In the late 1940s a group of cognitive psychologists, led by Benjamin Bloom, was looking for a way to help teachers improve their instruction.[3] The group was concerned that teachers only aimed at lower levels of cognition—the simple collection and regurgitation of basic information—while higher cognitive stages such as analyzing, critiquing, and creating were left unpursued. Facts and figures are the basic building blocks of knowledge, but Bloom and company wanted to encourage teachers to help students stretch well beyond the mere storehousing and retrieval of data. They should instead learn ways to assess it, apply it, and reconfigure it in new forms. The scholars wanted to help students understand and deal with the world in more true-to-life and productive ways. Bloom believed that staying at the lower end of the cognition scale was a great waste of educational opportunity and student potential. In addition to raising teachers' vision of what they taught, Bloom also wanted educators to find more precise ways of assessing outcomes to match those superior teaching aims.

What Bloom and his colleagues came up with was a taxonomy—an ordered list—that separated knowledge into six levels, from the most basic to the most intellectually challenging: **remember > understand > apply > analyze > evaluate > create**.

Here is a crash course in the taxonomy, intended not to make you an expert, but to demonstrate the *variety* of question options available to you as a storyteller. We'll introduce you to the taxonomy as an instructional tool (as it was originally developed), then show how you can draw from it as a storyteller. We begin at the bottom, with the simplest stage, then move up to higher levels of mental complexity.

Remember. The most basic level of questioning is designed to stimulate the recall of important facts, processes, or other data. This is useful at a basic level and sets the stage for more advanced exploration of a topic. We'll use nutrition as a sample subject.

How many main food groups are there? What are they?

What are some examples in each food group?

To begin, we're simply asking if they remember the basics of a topic.

Understand. Do listeners grasp the meaning of the subject? Do they get its purpose and importance?

Why do nutrition experts promote an understanding of food groups?

Why do they make recommendations about daily amounts in each group?

What is the point of having a "balanced diet"?

Notice that we've moved from asking them to recite correct answers to now demonstrating that they understand the topic.

Apply is the ability to put a concept to good use. Rather than just being able to understand something at the conceptual level (even deeply), can listeners see how it applies to themselves and others?

In what ways has your life been affected by modern nutritional information?

How have you changed your eating habits (if at all) due to your understanding of nutritional standards?

We're now asking them to take a concept or abstraction and use the information in real life.

Analyze is deeper. Can listeners think critically about the subject? Can they explore both its implications and ramifications?

Why have guidelines and definitions about nutrition changed over time?

What are the pros and cons of nutritional guidelines having evolved?

Now we ask them to delve down to a deeper level of examining the topic.

Evaluate is the ability to assess whether something is good or bad, right or wrong, and give reasons for your conclusions.

In what ways have nutritional guidelines improved people's health? Have there been any drawbacks? Explain.

What do you think about changes to food labeling laws based on new nutritional information? Explain.

This level requires them to not only understand and analyze the subject, but also make reasoned arguments for their particular perspective of it: take a stand and defend it.

Create is, in some ways, the most advanced kind of mental activity. It not only requires them to show that they understand and can apply an idea, but to come up with something different from what they started with. They go a step (or two) beyond where they began.

> *What would a meal high in protein and complex carbohydrates consist of?*

> *If you were to create a superfruit, what properties would it have? Which existing fruits could you combine to create it?*

A Tool to Avoid "Cricket Questions"

If you listen to a typical instructor or speaker trying to engage a group with questions, you'll likely hear many of what we call "cricket questions": so simple, obvious, or vague that the group does not answer. The room then becomes quiet enough that you can hear crickets chirping. It sound like this: "Zzzzzzz." (We could have called these "Zzzzzzzebra questions," but then we would lose the alliteration!) They're typically *remember* or *understand* questions, or just poorly designed queries. Here are some examples.

If I were teaching about this very subject—using questions to raise the level of teaching—I might ask:

"Are questions a good tool to use in your instruction?" (Answer: *Duh. Yes. Zzzzzzz*)

"Do you think you could create some good questions to stimulate learning?" (*Um, do you even need to ask? Do I really look incapable of creating good questions?*)

"When desiring a fuller exploitation of Bloom's Taxonomy, what intellectual levers may be activated to stimulate a higher pursuit of cognitive curiosity in learners, thus promoting more neural activity toward enrichment of academic achievement?" (*Whaaaat? I don't even understand what you're asking.*)

Okay, maybe you do understand it (because it does make sense) but will this type of question really help your audience want to think more deeply about your topic? (Rhetorical question; the answer is obvious.) This isn't teaching; it's showing off.

In addition to being low on the cognitive stimulation scale, you likely noticed that the first two examples are closed-ended questions. In general, these are weaker questions because they don't require much thought. *Um, yep. Mmmmm, sure. Hmmmm, I don't think so.* They're too obvious. Dull. Uninspiring. Soporific.

The last one is just plain pompous and convoluted. Rather than inviting listeners into the conversation, it serves only to showcase the speaker's impressive vocabulary—and unimpressive emotional intelligence.

Instead, when we teach, we typically want to ask *discovery* questions that require our listeners to ponder, searching for what they believe is the right answer, instead of being made to guess what *we* think is the one right answer. Here's what that might look like.

> "What types of questions tend to get your attention?"

> "How would *you* solve this dilemma?"

> "What key principles apply in this situation?"

Notice that one of the hallmarks of these questions is that they are directed to the listeners' experience, not the speaker's. Rather than launching questions that try to lead the listener to read your mind, they ask listeners to search their own minds to find answers. These questions create an internal locus of control, which increases their confidence. This leads to greater motivation, which creates positive emotions. These types of questions also acknowledge the intelligence and ability of your audience: They can do more than merely repeat what you've said; they can think on their own. All of this leads to greater attention, engagement, understanding, and retention.

At a minimum, we hope it's clear that these various types of questions represent different angles to approach a topic. They also require different levels of cognition to address them. In a word, they're *options* to stimulate listeners' thinking. You certainly don't have to use them all.

Applying Bloom's Taxonomy to Storytelling

All the advantages of questions as a teaching tool can be applied to our goals as storytellers. We can take a page out of Bloom's playbook for the classroom and adapt his taxonomy to stories. Our stories blossom and have maximum impact when we stretch our listeners by asking them — quite literally — to join us in the narrative.

The six levels give us options for engaging our audience in a variety of ways. You won't want to use all of them in a story — that would bog you down and make their brains explode — but the levels give you choices. Think of this as a menu from which you can choose. If you want a well-rounded meal, you likely would not pick from only the appetizer or dessert section of the menu (tempting as that might be). You'll want to make deliberate decisions about items from various parts of the menu that will round out your meal more fully. The same is true with Bloom's taxonomy: Choose the questions that will make your story more robust and engaging.

Level	Question Use	Example
Remember	Stimulates memory, not critical thinking. Use it to help recall important points right before teaching a concept.	*What skill was I planning to use?* *What was my major concern?* *What did I want to say?*
Understand	Check to see if the audience is tracking with you. Do they follow where the story is going?	*"Can you see why active listening helped in this case?"* *"What did I need to do before I replied?"*
Apply	Asks the audience to find ways to apply the point you're making.	*"What would you do next?"* *"Have you ever faced something like this? What did you do?"*
Analyze	Dig a little deeper. Can they think analytically about the situation?	*"What would you be thinking right about now?"* *"What do you think I did next?"* *"Which skill would help the most?"*
Evaluate	Listeners must assess the quality or value of something	*"How well do you think that worked for me? Why?"*

	based on reasons.	*"In your opinion, what would have been the best approach?"*
Create	The audience must come up with a novel answer; beyond applying or understanding, and identify a new way.	*"What else could I have tried?"* *"How could I have spoken up without losing my job?"*

Wait for it ...

One supporting skill to asking good discovery questions is the willingness to wait for a response. By definition, questions that inspire thought take time to answer. We realize that it can be painfully awkward to allow people the time — and silence — to consider your question, search their mental archives, then formulate a well-considered answer. But they're blazing new trails (at *your* invitation) and those new paths aren't formed instantly. Not allowing that development time does both you and them a disservice. It's demeaning to ask someone to do something difficult (like consider your brilliant question), then cut them off before they answer because you got antsy after a few seconds of quiet.

At first it may feel like the silence of a "cricket question," but something very different is happening. If the silence lasts longer than you can bear, and you're not sure if they're thinking or zoning out, reframe the question and ask it a different way. This sends the message that the silence is okay, and that you'll wait until they come up with their answer. Learn to live with the momentary awkwardness. You'll all be rewarded for your patience.

Closed-Ended Questions: A Word to the Wise

Having given all that adulation to open-ended discovery questions (and we stand by it), like all rules, there are exceptions—and this rule is no exception. (Wait. What?) When skillfully used, closed-ended, leading, and rhetorical questions can be your friends as a storyteller. It's all about the purpose to which you put them.

At times, you'll want to actively engage your audience in the story with you, so you'll want to use higher-level questions, the kind that both stimulate expansive thinking and practically demand an answer from your listeners. You're looking for real responses to your questions so as to create a richer story together. We'll call this the *teacher* mode. In this mode, you're encouraging others to think for themselves and explore ideas to find multiple interpretations and applications. You're asking them to join you actively in the story.

At other times, you want to tell the story without a lot of back-and-forth with your audience. You're just trying to make a point, illustrate a concept, or demonstrate the power of a skill. This is what we'll call the *teller* mode, and it's where closed and rhetorical questions work well. At these times, you'll focus on questions at the lower levels, just to spark some thought and mental engagement, not verbal answers, in your listeners.

The mode you select is typically a function of time, logistics, or purpose: how long you have for your story, how big your audience is, and what you're trying to accomplish with your story. If you're pressed for time, your audience is too big to engage with verbally, or you're just trying to illustrate a point, then you'll be more directive with your questions rather than exploratory. If, on the other hand, you have time to engage them, it's a relatively small group, and you want your point to sink in more, then asking more open-ended questions will draw them in and invite them to be co-creators with you in the experience the story helps to create.

These two modes have different objectives, and so call for different uses of questions. Here's what we mean.

If you're telling a story to *teach* a concept like freedom, you'll want to spur listeners' minds to consider what freedom means to them. You may want them to recall inspiring experiences that made them value their freedom, perhaps stories from heroes who have fought for their freedom and then used it for good. You may want listeners to explore the legal rights that grant certain freedoms to citizens, and the legitimate limits on those rights. So, you'd want to ask questions like:

> *"How well do our country's laws enable citizens to speak freely?"*
>
> *"Which historical figures inspire your respect for what they did to promote freedom?"*
>
> *"In your opinion, how might civil liberties and governmental/military needs clash? How would you resolve that tension?"*

These are all questions that require careful analysis, contemplation, and insight in order to answer. That is good instructional design.

By contrast, in *teller* mode, you have a particular angle in mind — it's why you're telling the story. Rather than stimulating creative thought, you're simply illustrating a point.

For example, you may want to recount the experience of an ancestor who fled adverse conditions in the old country and traveled to a new land seeking a better life. You'd tell about the aspirations and travails of this ancestor. Along the way, you could use questions to engage your audience, but you're not asking your listeners to analyze the situation or come up with their own conclusions about it. Instead, you're just asking them to listen carefully and understand. So, you may say:

> "In 1726, my fifth great-grandfather, Heinrich Adam Hermann, fled famine and war in southwest Germany to create a new life in the United States. He was just twenty-six years old. His young family braved weeks on a ship crossing the Atlantic and settled in a land where they did not speak the language, just to have the freedom to start their lives over. *How important must freedom have been to them to risk so much?*"

Using a rhetorical question here stimulates the listeners to consider the mindset of Heinrich and his family. It's not really asking them to give an answer, but it invites their rapt attention by putting them in his shoes (or skull) as it were. Rhetorical questions help you drive home or reiterate an important point, but don't require a verbal response.

You could also use a closed-ended question to accomplish this, one that has only one correct answer:

"Wouldn't you want the opportunity to pursue your life free from starvation and war?"

The answer is obvious, but you can use it to make a point in the form of a question. Both of these are effective ways to engage listeners in your story.

So, at moments of decision, crisis, or summary in your story you can interject a question to pique the audience by drawing out their answers, either verbally or mentally. You can begin with a simple question to keep them hooked on the story like, "Have you ever felt that way?" or "Have you ever found yourself in a similar situation?" These are easy to answer and are designed to simply awaken the listener out of a passive state. When someone mentally replies, "Oh, yeah," they've moved from passive to active participant in your story.

Key Points

- Questions supply an additional way to enhance your stories. They invite audience participation in several ways. Questions stimulate the brain and turn a passive experience into an active collaboration. They also break your story into smaller chunks and give your audience time to digest it. Questions are irresistible.

- In *teller* mode, closed and rhetorical questions draw out mental answers and work well when you're short on time, have an audience too big to effectively engage in dialogue, or keep your story moving when you're just illustrating a point.

- In *trainer* mode, open questions actively invite listeners to participate in the story. They stimulate higher mental states and allow space for listeners to help you make the points of the story. Use these in smaller groups when you have the time and when the learning point is deeper or more important to get across to your audience. Both types of questions can be effective when used deliberately. If you want listeners to answer, make that clear by providing a prompt: "Who has an idea or experience to share?"

- Like stories themselves, you can get a lot of mileage from good, engaging questions. The key is to be deliberate about the different types of questions you use. Watch out for the common trap of only asking lower-level questions (remember and understand) during your stories—you don't want to hear crickets! Tap into the power of questions to get your listeners more deeply engaged in your stories, which will help them understand, remember, and apply the points you're making.

Application

Go back to the story you outlined in the last chapter. Apply the power of questions to your story:

1. Find a few places within your story to draw in the audience with questions.

2. Consider the different questions you could ask. Which would be most helpful to engage your audience and appropriately draw them into your story?

    - What do you notice about the various types of questions? What stands out to you about their differences? How could this insight help you select the best question(s)?

    - Try to create a good mix of different types of questions to ask.

3. Come up with a good call-to-action question or request to end your story.

4. Level Up: Once you're feeling comfortable using questions deliberately, you can take the next step up in your skill and use these questions in both **teller** *and* **teacher** modes: first to simply get them thinking, then to stimulate thoughtful discussion.

Six: Finish Your Story by …

At this point, you should have a story outlined that has a specific purpose — to teach, lead, inspire, etc. You've identified some questions to engage your audience and bring them into your experience. Now you're ready to deliver, right?

Almost.

This chapter gives a few cautions to consider and some pointers around practicing your story. Even the best-outlined story will benefit from some deliberate practice. In addition to identifying any gaps in your story, practice gives you the confidence that your story is solid, and that you know how to deliver it.

Let's be clear: not every storytelling situation deserves copious practice. If you're having dinner with friends and want to tell about that time you asked Ryan Reynolds for an autograph and told him he was great in "The Notebook" because you confused him with Ryan Gosling, you probably don't need to step away from the meal to rehearse. Or if you want to illustrate a quick point in a team meeting about working together by sharing how Amanda helped you out recently, you shouldn't put it on the agenda for next week's gathering in order to get some prep time.

But if you're giving a speech, teaching a class, going to an interview, or preparing for any big event where a story will help, invest the time to practice storytelling. The more you practice storytelling, the better you'll get at telling those stories in the moment, too.

Don't worry, you won't need a professional coach to get valuable practice. (Of course, if you *want* a professional coach, you can find some at www.MasterStorytelling.com.) Be careful not to underestimate the value of getting the words out of your mouth in a low-risk setting before you stand in front of an audience, where it really counts.

More on practice in a few pages. First, the cautions.

A Few Cautions on Delivery

Even the best story can lose impact without the right delivery. Remember the novice storyteller in prison? We're not suggesting you have to be the perfect orator or a stand-up comic in order to effectively use storytelling. But there are a few distractions that can get in the way of a well-designed story hitting the mark. Watch out for these common slips.

The Dreaded Filler Words

One of my college professors had difficulty finishing a sentence without at least one "uh" or "um" or the great combination "uh-um." During one 50-minute lecture, I put a tick mark at the top of my notes every time he said one of those words. The tally was over 200 when I gave up counting. Looking back, the more important tally was how little I actually got out of the lecture! I was so busy counting the fillers that I didn't absorb the topic of discussion.

You've likely heard something similar, and maybe you've done it yourself (but probably not to the extreme of my professor—after all, he was a *professional*). We all have "filler" words that we use when we're feeling a little uncomfortable or nervous or get a little lost in our stories. The technical term for them is "disfluencies"—an interruption in the smooth flow of speech.

These filler words also break the flow of your story. They're more than just the full stop of punctuation—they're a detour. When you say, "uh…" or "um," your listeners have to stop processing your story and wait for what comes next. At a minimum, that's slightly annoying. You want to keep your audience engaged, and if they're distracted by the disfluencies, you could lose them (think about me in my college class). In addition, as you use your stories to teach, lead, and inspire, your message needs to be easy to follow and understand. If they're lost in your "uhs" and "ums," your listeners could lose the point you're trying to make.

Some of our disfluencies are sounds like *uh* or *um* or *ah* or even *mm*. Others are perfectly good words in certain situations, but when they get repeated too often they become distracting. These words can include *like, and, now, okay, so,* among others. We're not suggesting you can never use these words or phrases, just use them for their intended purpose and not as fillers.

My favorite filler words are *so* and *okay* and *now*. What's your favorite?

If you don't know what your filler words are, ask a trusted friend or colleague. They probably hear your filler words in your day-to-day speech patterns. If they don't, that's a good sign for you. Maybe you don't use them too frequently, or maybe your friends have simply gotten used to your fillers. Don't count on that for your story audience.

Experts suggest that instead of the filler word, teach yourself to pause briefly.[1] Because your brain can process speech so quickly, a two-second pause can seem exceptionally long for you. But a pause allows you to collect yourself and breathe and audiences perceive speakers who pause as more confident and in control. Embrace the pause as a replacement for the disfluencies.

While you want to avoid saying these filler words repeatedly, don't get paranoid about never using any. They're going to slip out on occasion, which makes your speech natural. According to research by Quantified Communications, the optimum frequency is about one filler per minute, but the average speaker uses five fillers per minute (one every 12 seconds).[2] I don't think my college professor was in this study; he would have skewed that number higher! So don't worry about "that word" when it slips into your story once in a while. That's normal. If you're so concerned about it that you grimace or lose your place in the story because you said "that word," it's worse than saying the word!

Phrases to Avoid

Some disfluencies are more than pauses — they are filler phrases. We sometimes hear people use these phrases casually, which means they don't hear the message it sends to their audience. Here are a some of the phrases that make us cringe (you may be able to think of others) and why we see them as problematic:

"To be honest" or "honestly" What, you haven't been honest up to this point?

"Believe me" If you have to tell someone to believe you, maybe your message isn't that credible. People should be able to believe you without your command to believe you.

"You know?" or "Right?" It sounds like a rhetorical question when you use this phrase. People use this to ensure their listeners are tracking with them or to emphasize a point they're making. It's okay in small doses, but if you use it frequently, the impact is gone.

"Obviously" If it's obvious, you shouldn't have to call out that it's obvious. This word can sound to listeners like, "In case you're too dull to get this, let me tell you." There are appropriate uses of the word obvious, but using it at the beginning of a sentence can come across as condescending — obviously.

"Kinda, sorta, maybe" We hear these a lot. Someone is telling a story about a challenging situation. "My coworker promised to represent us in a meeting with leadership. We *kinda* talked about what we wanted and how he would make our case. Then the next day, I *sort of* find out he didn't go to the meeting and, as a result, we *kinda* didn't get any budget for our project. When I asked him about it he said, 'Well, it's *sort of* your fault for not being available. Why are you putting this all on me?' I was *kinda* upset."

Hmmm. Kinda talked? Kinda didn't get budget? Kinda upset? The use of kinda diminishes the power of the sentence. I think in most instances "kinda" is a filler word. But it has a more negative impact than most fillers. Have a friend or coach listen for this word (or listen for it when you record yourself). Leave it out. It's kinda useless.

"Literally" I heard someone leading a class share an experience when she was afraid she was going to lose her job and potentially ruin her career. As she got to the climax of the story she said, "I literally died on the spot." Uh, no. If she had "literally" died, she wouldn't be alive to tell the story — unless the next part of the story was that she got CPR to revive her (and it wasn't). Please, we beg you, only use *literally* when you really mean it literally.

"Irregardless" and other non-words. In case you've used this one, the word is "regardless" (or "irrespective" if you use big words). You don't have to be a perfect grammarian, but don't use made-up words. They get in the way of the point. A coach or friend can point these out to you in practice. (More on practice to come soon.)

Internal Dialogue

I was listening to a speaker tell of a personal experience. He had a good story that made an important point, but it was almost unbearable to listen to. For starters, he didn't follow the tips for what makes a good story that we outlined in chapter 3. The bigger issue was that he interrupted himself multiple times to share the random thoughts that passed through his head at the moment.

"We were at the lake wakeboarding. It was a beautiful day. I think it was a Thursday. No, maybe a Tuesday. My friend Jeff was with us along with his wife. I've forgotten her name. It might have been something like Karen or Theresa. No, I think it was Brenda."

I'm squirming in my seat thinking, "I don't care what your friend's wife's name is. Get to the point!"

The brain works much faster than our mouths do. We will always have thoughts that go beyond what we're sharing in our stories. Keep them in your brain where they belong and stick to only the relevant points of your story that help convey your message.

The most common violation of this I hear is when people say, "Oops, I forgot something." Or "Oh, I messed that up." Sure, you'll forget things. Sure, you'll mess up at times. But guess what? The people listening to you won't know it—unless you tell them!

Instead, train yourself to either pause or switch that internal script to a purposeful external script. You can insert a forgotten part by saying something like, "Now, you need to understand that before this happened, ..." and simply fold the forgotten part into the narrative as though you intended it to come at that point all along. Then, the next time you tell that story, put it where you originally intended it to be. Practice brings polish.

Vocal Variation

My mother used to repeat a phrase to me on a regular basis—usually when I was arguing with one of my siblings. Even if your mother didn't use this phrase, I'm sure you've heard it from someone. I'll start the phrase and you finish it:

> "It's not what you say ..."

Whenever I bring this up, at least 90 percent of the people finish with "... it's how you say it." That's what my mom used to tell me.

But with storytelling, it's both what you say *and* how you say it. We talked in chapter 3 about what to say. Now let's talk briefly about how you say it.

Be sure to vary your vocal inflections, volume, and pace as you deliver your story. Comedian Steven Wright delivers everything in a deadpan monotone. (If you're not familiar with him, look him up on YouTube.) He says things like, "I put a skylight in my place; the people in the apartment above me hate it" without so much as cracking a smile (and barely moving his lips). Part of the reason it's funny is because his delivery is so unnatural. It's part of his schtick, his comedic routine. It's not for everyone. In fact, it's not for *anyone*, except Steven Wright.

As you're building up to the conflict, you might want to quicken your pace a bit. When you're making the learning point, slow down. When there were strong emotions expressed, your volume will likely be a little louder. When you're telling something you were thinking, it might come out softer.

I've told a story about getting upgraded to first class on a flight home from a business trip. Wahoo! This is a rare occasion! I'm going to love the extra leg room and elbow room. (When I talk about the upgrade, my voice gets a little louder and higher. Hey, it's exciting!)

I sit down in first class and realize I've got a bunch of great free movies I could watch. The guy next to me already has his headphones on watching *Minority Report*, so I start looking for the headphone jack. I can't find it. (I get quieter here; it's embarrassing that I can't find something as simple as a headphone jack!)

I try to subtly look at my neighbor to see where he's plugged his headphones in. I don't want to ask him; I'd look stupid! And I can't ask a flight attendant; if they know I can't find a simple headphone jack they might kick me out of first class! (Can you hear that phrase getting a little animated?)

Finally, I realize that my internal dialogue is getting ridiculous. (Now my volume and pitch come to a calmer point to emphasize that I'm finally being rational.) I stop the flight attendant and say, "I'm sorry to bother you. I can't figure out where the headphone jack is." The flight attendant smiles and says, "This happens all the time. This is a newer plane. The headphone jack is behind your right shoulder."

No big deal. I plug in my headphone jack, and they didn't kick me out of first class. (I say this as a stage whisper, kind of our little secret.) My seatmate watches as I plug in my headphone jack, pulls off his headphones, and says, "Thanks for asking that. I couldn't figure out where the headphone jack was either" and he plugs in his headphones. He'd been watching *Minority Report* as a *silent movie* this whole time because he wasn't willing to ask either! (The animation goes up for this last line.)

The point is this: How many times do we talk ourselves out of speaking up about something because our internal voice tells us it's going to go badly? The reality is that when we speak up, we get what we need sooner, and we're likely helping other people at the same time. (This is delivered a little slower and in a calm voice to bring the point home.)

I called out for you where and how my voice changed through that story, but as a reader, you could probably pick up where the changes were. Don't just *say* your story; *tell* your story. Your voice can convey the emotions, keep the listener interested, and help drive home the point.

Pay attention to people who are good storytellers. Listen not only to their structure but to when they change volume, pitch, and pace (except Steven Wright). Again, practicing these more subtle inclusions will benefit you greatly.

Move Your Body

I was sitting around a table with four other people who were there to judge me. Literally! I was sitting for a certification to teach a course. I needed to pass this certification in order to do my job, so the stakes were high. The four people around the table were tasked with grilling me to make sure I knew what I was doing. They asked probing questions, interrogated me on how I would handle objections from the class, and made me dive into the finer details of the course content.

Then they asked me to tell a story to illustrate one of the concepts of the class. Whew! Now I'm in my element. I love telling stories. I was still nervous—after all, the jury would be deliberating after all of this was over. I started telling my story but found myself stumbling around the key points and not sounding smooth. It took me about 30 seconds to figure out what was wrong.

I paused and asked, "Can I stand up to tell this story?" They agreed. I stood up and started over. Everything went smoothly after that. I couldn't tell the story sitting down, because I felt restricted in my body movement. The story included my walking over to someone, so when I tell the story, I usually walk across the room as I'm telling that part of the story.

When telling your stories, get your body involved. Your gestures, movements, expressions, etc. will help make the point of your story. You've likely heard of studies that say our words are a small percentage of what we communicate. Nonverbals like tone of voice, facial expressions, and body language communicate much more than the words alone do.

Having said that, you don't need to run around, jump up and down, and gesticulate wildly to get your points across. Move in ways that emphasize your key points. For example, lean forward when making a subtle point, as though you're sharing a secret with your audience. Slump your shoulders as you explain how you made a mistake. Stand tall when you achieved the victory! Let your body support what you're saying.

Sometimes our nerves take our bodies one way or the other. We get nervous and we freeze, hardly making any movement. Conversely, some people get overly animated and speak too loudly when the nerves kick in. Look for the balance that helps communicate what you're saying without nonverbally saying something you don't intend.

I've heard the advice that when you get nervous you should look over the heads of your audience and pretend they're not there. (I've also heard to picture your audience naked, which is ridiculous to me because I would be more nervous standing in front of a room of naked people!) The problem with the "look over their heads" advice is that you lose your connection with your audience.

The more you can make eye contact, the more your audience will connect with your story. Look at them as though you're telling your story to a friend. They'll listen more and relate better to your story than if you're looking at the floor or the ceiling. If you happen to be giving a presentation in a darkened room where you cannot see the faces of your audience, you should still look to where they're sitting. Looking into the dark void takes some practice, but the people in the seats will sense you're looking in their eyes even if you can't see them. As a result, they'll stay more connected to you.

If it makes you nervous or distracts you to look in people's eyes directly, try this trick: Look at their eyebrows. As odd as that may sound, looking at people's eyebrows while speaking takes away the intimidation you may feel by looking directly into their eyes. At the same time, it looks to your audience as if you're looking right into their eyes, giving you the benefit of connection we mentioned above.

One final point on body language. When you're making your point—that moment when the story conveys the message you want people to hear—stand still. That's the moment you want people to focus on your words only. The contrast between moving and gesturing while telling the story then standing still at the conclusion will help listeners focus on and remember your key points.

How to Practice

I had an experience that I was sure would effectively teach a point. I thought through how I would deliver it. In my head, it sounded great. I shared the illustration with my wife. When I finished, she looked at me blankly and said, "I don't get it." I thought through the story again and realized it didn't have the impact I initially expected. I never used the story to try to illustrate the concept.

Feedback is a gift. If I hadn't gotten the feedback from my wife, I likely would have tried that story in a professional setting and it would have flopped. Would that have ruined my career? Probably not. But I would have missed an opportunity to be impactful with a different story.

Whatever level of experience you have as a presenter, facilitator, leader, coach, or any other capacity in which you will use stories, you will benefit from practicing. And rehearsing the story in your head does NOT count as practice. (See my story above for evidence!) You have to get the words out of your mouth, especially the questions you plan to ask, to ensure your story has the necessary components and the flow you expect.

Here are some suggestions on practicing your stories.

Phone a Friend

For your first practice, use a friend—a trusted colleague, a family member, someone you know cares about you as a person. The reason we recommend this is because you want to feel safe. With a friend, you know they have your best interests at heart, so you don't need to worry about feeling embarrassed or put down when you get feedback.

At the same time, make it clear to your friend that you *expect* feedback. You *want* feedback. You don't want them to gloss over problems or merely tell you what they think you want to hear. A real friend will want to help, and that includes giving some corrective instruction when needed.

The First Time

If you aren't accustomed to using storytelling to convey your messages, this is an important tip for you. The first time you practice your story, ask your friend/coach to only give you *positive* feedback. Cue your coach to answer these questions:

> What did you like most about the story?
>
> What did you see as the main point of the story?

The reason we suggest this "positive only" feedback rule when you're starting out as a storyteller is that we want you to experience the sense of success. If you get negative feedback to start, you may get discouraged and give up on storytelling. There's no need for you to do that. If you've followed the outline we've given you in this book, you'll have some good elements to your story. Feed off of those positives to strengthen your storytelling skills.

Now Go Deeper

After you've had more experience—or after you've practiced the story with some positive feedback—it's time to go deeper on your feedback. But don't go deeper on feedback until you're ready to get that feedback. Keep in mind that feedback is a gift. Even if it isn't given in the best way, remember that the purpose of feedback is to improve your storytelling. It's not personal, so don't take it that way.

Have you ever been given a present that wasn't wrapped well? (If you are or have been a parent of 10-year-old, the answer is almost certainly yes.) The wrapping doesn't make the gift any less valuable or the love of the giver any less sincere. The feedback you get may not be wrapped in the most beautiful language. But it's still a gift with value and coming from a place of caring and helpfulness.

Feedback is a snapshot in time about your performance *then*. Negative feedback doesn't define you as a person or as a storyteller. It's simply what happened in *that* instance of telling the story. Once you improve your performance, you go beyond where you've been, and that feedback no longer represents you. You're now new and improved!

When you're ready, ask your coach to answer *some* of the following questions:

> What problems did you see in the story?
>
> Were there enough details to be clear?
>
> Did any details seem unnecessary?
>
> Was the story long enough/too long?
>
> Were there points that could have been made that I didn't make?
>
> Were there any logic gaps in the story?
>
> What could make the story flow better?

You can come up with your own questions as well, but these are some that may prompt useful responses. You could also have a coach stop you during your story to correct anything that doesn't seem clear.

Check Your Disfluencies

If you find yourself struggling with disfluencies and filler words, practice with the purpose of finding and reducing those words and phrases. For a real eye-opener (and we recommend this) have someone listen to your story and count how many times you use filler words. If you don't know what your filler words are, this is another way to find out. You'll likely be surprised at how high the tally rises. More than anything else, it will bring your awareness up.

Then tell the story again to your practice partner and have them snap their fingers or tap the table or clear their throat every time you use the word. This will help you be conscious about *when* you use the words in addition to *what* words you tend to overuse.

Another twist on this is to record yourself telling a story, then listen for filler words and sounds. You'll also find words, phrases, and inflections that get in the way of your story. Once you've identified those issues, record yourself again. Compare your tally of fillers on the second try to your first. If the number is still high, try again. Sometimes listening to yourself on a recording can be painful (it is for me), but this will give you instant data.

Largely, you can structure the practice in whatever way helps you feel more comfortable telling your story before you deliver it to your intended audience. As you get better at storytelling, you'll have more focused practices. But even experienced storytellers benefit from practicing before delivering to an audience. After some experience, you'll find that as you practice your stories, you will catch many of the problems yourself. Still, practice. It's the best way to ensure your story will have the impact you desire.

And Now ...

So, here we are at the end ... but also at the beginning. This is the beginning of your journey as a storyteller, or the next level up in your progression as a storyteller. You're not going to need every single point made in this book for every story you use to teach, lead, or inspire. But please always remember the premise we started with.

You *are* a storyteller.

You have a lifetime of experiences to draw from, and more on the way. By converting these experiences into meaningful stories, you can have a greater impact on your audiences. You may not need storytelling for every instance that you need to convey a message. When the trash is overflowing, you don't need to find an illustration of the powerful impact of removing waste from your home or office. Just tell someone to take out the garbage (or do it yourself). But there will be other times when you'll want to share facts, data, and other information to convey some point, and you now have a powerful way to make those facts come to life. Bring in a story to illustrate, illuminate, or motivate when sharing data alone won't move people to action.

I once heard our friend (and foreword writer) Ron McMillan say:

> One of the most powerful things you can do to be an effective speaker is to use stories to touch people's minds and hearts. By telling heartfelt stories, people not only get the idea you're trying to make mentally, but they feel something in their hearts as well. They associate with experiences they've had, and that tends to validate what you're telling them in the story.[3]

We hope you see how storytelling is another powerful option in your efforts to influence others. Your life is full of experiences you can use. Keep looking for them. Take note when you find them. Craft them deliberately so they have the greatest impact on your listeners. Don't expect to be perfect, but keep using stories and you'll get better.

Do you remember the first time you tried to use a new software program? Maybe the first time you created a formula in a spreadsheet or tried to create a graphic in a design program? It probably wasn't pretty. The program may have seemed awkward and uncomfortable. The result wasn't what you expected.

You may have been given some guidance on how to use the program more effectively and, over time, you got more comfortable and your results improved.

The same thing will happen with your storytelling. Keep working on it. Don't give up if a story falls flat the first time or two. Look back on the structure we provided in this book. What was missing in your story? What could you have done better? Try it again. Or, if you decide the story doesn't really work, let it go and apply what you learned to find another experience and create another story.

But never give up. Stories carry too much power to abandon them. Whatever role you play in business or in your personal life, you have opportunities to teach, lead, and inspire. Stories can help you do that more effectively.

Near the end of the novel *The Night Circus*, author Erin Morgenstern includes a brief dialogue that reinforces our message. The book is about people with special abilities who form a magical traveling circus. The character Widget was born into the circus and is explaining his special skill.

> "You tell stories?" the man asks, the piquing of his interest almost palpable.
>
> "Stories, tales, bardic chronicles," Widget says. "Whatever you care to call them. The things we

were discussing earlier that are more complicated than they used to be. I take pieces of the past that I see and I combine them into narratives. It's not that important, and this isn't why I'm here—"

"It *is* important," the man in the grey suit interrupts. "Someone needs to tell those tales. When the battles are fought and won and lost, when the pirates find their treasures and the dragons eat their foes for breakfast with a nice cup of Lapsang souchong, someone needs to tell their bits of overlapping narrative. There's magic in that. It's in the listener, and for each and every ear it will be different, and it will affect them in ways they can never predict. From the mundane to the profound. You may tell a tale that takes up residence in someone's soul, becomes their blood and self and purpose. That tale will move them and drive them and who knows what they might do because of it, because of your words. This is your role, your gift. Your sister may be able to see the future, but you yourself can shape it, boy. Do not forget that." He takes another sip of his wine. "There are many kinds of magic, after all."

Remember, you *are* a storyteller. Tell your stories. Make your magic.

Key Points

Now that you've identified experiences to use, crafted them into stories with powerful questions, and selected how you will use these stories, here are a few points to remember as you tell your stories:

- When you deliver your story:
    - Watch out for filler words
    - Quiet your internal dialogue
    - Add interest with vocal variations
    - Engage your body, using appropriate gestures and movements

- Practice your stories when preparing for important presentations, meetings, interviews, etc.
    - Get feedback from friends
    - Record yourself
    - Keep practicing

- Now it's up to you. Start creating and sharing your stories. There's magic in that!

Application

Now that you've got an experience converted into a story, take the following steps to use that story to teach, lead, and inspire.

1. **Practice.** Get a coach (a friend, family member, trusted colleague, etc.) and ask them to listen to the story. Have them tell you what they liked and what they thought was the main point of the story.

2. **Practice more.** Refine the story based on the feedback from your first practice. Then have someone listen to the story and go deeper on the feedback:
- What was good? What could improve?

- Were there any gaps in the story?

- Was it long enough to include sufficient detail but not so long that you lost the listener?

- Develop other questions to improve your story and give them to your coach to answer after hearing your story.

3. **Get detailed.** Watch out for disfluencies or filler words and phrases. Either have a coach identify those as they listen to you or record yourself and listen to them yourself.

4. **Set a date.** When and where will you use your story? Set a time by which you will try out what you learned from this book. Then do it!

5. **Do it again.** Find more experiences to turn into purposeful stories. Look for opportunities to use your storytelling skills. Keep practicing, keep growing, keep benefiting from these skills.

Appendix: Story Examples

If you're still struggling to come up with stories of your own, the following pages include some sample stories. Before you read these stories, here are a few ways you could use them as you develop your storytelling prowess:

1) As illustrations that might get you thinking about some of your own experiences you could use to teach, lead, and inspire. You may read these stories and think, "That reminds of the time when …" and voilà! You've got your own story.

2) As an exercise to help you think about how you might apply your stories. We've included some questions at the end of each story. These questions are designed to get you thinking about how stories can teach, lead, and inspire. These questions may also give you good questions to consider when crafting your own stories to make them most impactful.

3) To borrow while you're developing your own stories. Remember, using other people's stories to make a point is okay. Your own stories will be more powerful because you'll have the emotional connection to them. But if you can't come up with any of your own and one of the stories below helps you illustrate a point you want to make, go ahead and borrow it. Don't try to make it sound like the experience actually happened to you, but tell it as, "In a book I read recently, they told about ..."

4) For fun. We hope you enjoy some of the stories below and they show you the impact a good story can have as you teach, lead, and inspire.

Without further ado, here are a few stories for your consideration and enjoyment.

Trouble With Teams

For 10 years, I taught a college course as an adjunct professor. On the first day of each semester, I could count on students in my class groaning over one announcement: "One-third of your grade will be based on team projects."

While it may not be as overt, I think the same sentiment often exists in the work environment. "We'd like you to join the cross-functional team for the Periwinkle Unicorn project." (Internal groan) "Okay, sure." (Sigh.)

And what's the main complaint, both in the college course and at work? The college version is, "I end up doing more work than other members of the team, so either they get credit for my work or everyone suffers because of the slackers." Hmmm. Sounds about the same at work, doesn't it?

One semester, three members of a five-person team approached me after class to tell me about the problems with one teammate I'll call Jana. They complained that Jana was dragging the team down, not working hard or contributing much. They were worried that Jana would drag their grade down and wanted to get rid of her. They rated her work on a recent project extremely low — 20% total contribution — which would affect Jana's grade.

My first question to the three team members was, "Have you talked to her about these problems?" Want to guess the answer? You've got a 50/50 chance of getting it right, but you probably don't even need those odds. No. They hadn't said anything. I'm guessing there were some terse emails and withering looks, but no conversation—at least not with Jana.

I gave a few suggestions about how they could bring the issue up with Jana, particularly focusing on specific examples of where she was letting them down.

I emailed Jana to let her know that her teammates had rated her participation low on the last assignment. (I did not mention the after-class meeting.) Jana was stunned. Her perspective was that members of the team were withholding information and leaving her out of important decisions. She was trying to contribute more in the background because that's what she thought her team wanted from her. But had she ever asked them about how she could best contribute? You guessed it—nope.

The two sides talked, and by the next assignment, everyone was happy with the contributions of everyone else on the team. The only real magic was opening their mouths and respectfully sharing their views. Sure, they had talked before about their projects, but they never talked about how they were working together. By the end of the semester, they all got good grades and had become friends as well.

Application: *If you want to use this story, consider the following questions:*

> How can you apply this story to the teams you're working on?
>
> How could you apply the story as a team leader? As a team member?
>
> What different messages come out of this story for you?
>
> What points would you want to emphasize to get that message across?
>
> Does this story remind you of any experiences you've had with teams that may be useful in illustrating an important message?

Run Home

When my oldest son was 6 years old, I volunteered to help coach his coed T-ball team. None of these kids went on to major league baseball careers, but we tried to teach them the fundamentals of the game, some specific skills, and teamwork.

Keeping in mind the size and skills of these players, the fielding positions were a little different than regular baseball. Even the best hitters rarely got the ball out of the infield. One player stayed near each base. The "outfielders" played on the edge of the base paths. Two players flanked the pitcher in the infield.

During one game when our team was in the field, the other team loaded the bases. We had no outs against them. One girl—I'll call her Kallee—was playing a short infield position where many of the hit balls were coming. I said to her, "Kallee, if the ball comes to you, run up and step on home plate." Kallee dutifully nodded.

What happened on the very next play? Sure enough, the next hit came directly to her. She sprinted to home plate, stomped on the rubber mat, and looked to me proudly. Of course, she never picked up the ball, so the opposing player scored.

I couldn't get upset with her. She did exactly what I told her to do. Instead, I said to Kallee, "Good job. You did just what I told you. Next time, if the ball comes to you, *pick it up*, then run and step on home plate." Kallee nodded, and on the next play we got the out. And we both learned from the experience.

Has that ever happened to you? You assumed someone knew what you were thinking. Hey, it's common sense based on your experience. Everyone knows how to do this, don't they?

I had fallen into what Chip and Dan Heath call "the curse of knowledge" in their book, *Made to Stick: Why Some Ideas Survive and Others Die*. The curse of knowledge is the human tendency to assume that everyone else knows what we know. The knowledge we have makes some things seem obvious to us, and we can't understand why they aren't obvious to others. I assumed that Kallee would know that in order to get an out, she needed to have the ball in her hand or glove.

The same thing can happen at work. I once asked a new employee—let's call him Sam—to write an article for a newsletter. I gave what I thought were clear instructions, we agreed on the deadline, I asked if he had questions, and he went on his way to complete the assignment.

When I got the first draft, it was completely off target—from my perspective. I couldn't believe it! I'd hired this guy because I thought he was a skilled writer. Now I would have to take a lot of extra time to fix this inadequate effort. At this point, how do you think I was feeling? Yep, the frustration was mounting.

I called him into my office to review the differences between what he gave me and what I expected. He was stunned, and a little embarrassed. But the fault was not all his. I have to take some responsibility for the "curse of knowledge" getting in my way. I assumed he understood what was in my head without being clear. He was new to the industry, and I knew that. I failed to take his perspective into consideration or ask more probing questions when giving the initial instructions.

Sometimes we forget that not everyone has played the game as long as we have. Clear instructions lead to clear results. Fight the curse of knowledge by considering the background of others and getting feedback on your instructions. Then win the game—together.

Application: *If you were to use this story, consider the following questions:*

> What are some ways "the curse of knowledge" has affected you? Could you share an experience of your own instead of these examples?
>
> What can you do to overcome "the curse of knowledge"? What would you like people to do differently once they hear this story?

How could you use this story to teach or inspire your team? What challenges could this illustration help your team overcome?

What are some additional points you could make about "the curse of knowledge" that would be helpful to your audience?

Ethical Emergency

I'd been working for a small technology company—by small I mean 25 people—for about six months when I faced an interesting dilemma. I was preparing a press release for the launch of a new version of our primary product. The last person on the approval list for the press release was the CEO, who was one of the co-founders of the company.

The CEO—we'll call him Chad—called me into his office after he reviewed the release. He said, "There's an important piece missing," and went on to describe a technical feature that no one else had brought up in the review process. I asked a few clarifying questions, then added a paragraph to the press release.

Chad reviewed the paragraph and said it was accurate. I decided before finalizing the release to ask the chief technology officer—the other co-founder of the company—to review the paragraph to ensure it was technically accurate. After reading the paragraph, he said, "Why did you add this paragraph?"

"Chad said it needed to be included," I replied.

The CTO, whom I'll call Ed, shook his head. "Nope," he said. "That feature isn't in this version of the product. We're hoping to develop it for the next version, but we're not even 100 percent sure we can do it."

I figured Chad must have misunderstood, so I went back to the CEO and said, "Ed tells me that feature isn't in this version of the product, so I'm going to take that paragraph out of the press release."

Chad's response was, "I know it's not in this version, but leave the paragraph in. Just make it sound defensible."

Defensible? I wasn't even sure what he meant by that, so I asked.

He explained, "Write it in a way that if anyone asks us about it we can say we really meant it was going to be in the next version. This is a really important feature that will make us stand out from the competition. It needs to be in there."

I said, "I don't think that's a good idea. That could really come back to haunt us." I was trying to protect the company and him … and myself! I would be the one who had to "defend" the statement.

Chad's eyes narrowed and his voice raised. "Look," he said, "you work for me. I sign the paychecks. You do what I tell you to do. Now get out."

What do you think was going through my head at this time? What would you be thinking? I had a family of three small children at the time. Was I supposed to sacrifice my job or my integrity?

In hindsight, I can think of all sorts of things I could have said. In the moment, though, I said nothing. After a moment of hesitation—in which Chad turned his back to me—I went back to my office. My head was spinning.

It took me about 15 minutes to decide what to do next. I went back to Ed's office and said, "I need your help." I explained what had happened with Chad, and Ed immediately stood up and said, "Nope, that's not going to happen."

He went back with me to the CEO's office and talked Chad out of that decision. I removed the paragraph from the press release, and then what do you think I did next?

If you guessed "updated your resume and started applying for new jobs" you'd be right. Within three months, I was off to another company. Looking back, I wonder if, with better skills, I could have handled the situation better, stayed at the company, and helped the CEO and others be more successful.

Application: *If you want to use this story, consider the following questions:*

> What are the lessons you take away from this story? What lessons could this story teach? Who needs to hear this story?

The story is from one perspective, but what are the perspectives of others in the story? What do you learn from Chad and Ed?

How could this story be about correcting behavior? And whose behavior?

Meeting Mistake

It was the worst possible timing to make a simple mistake. The startup software company I was working for was transitioning to a new CEO, someone coming in from the outside to get the company ready for an IPO or a merger. I was responsible for setting up the first company-wide meeting to allow the CEO to introduce himself and set his agenda.

I'd set up half a dozen of these types of meetings for this company in the past, the most recent one about four months previously. We used a large meeting hall in the building adjacent to us in the business park where the home office was located. This accommodated the 125 employees who worked at headquarters, then we connected the 40 remote and international employees via a Web connection.

The management of the meeting room had changed hands, but they reserved the time for us and confirmed the space was available the following week. It was a short turnaround, so I was relieved we found an open time. But I forgot to double-check to make sure the technology was still the same. I assumed that the Internet connection was available as it had always been in the past.

You can probably guess what happened. On the morning of the meeting, I got there to set up and there was no Internet connection. I got hold of the people who manage the room and asked if we could connect to the Internet. They said, "Oh, no one ever uses the Internet in that room, so we took out all the connections." I was sick. We tried to find other options to make it work, but couldn't get a connection anywhere.

Our workaround was to record the session and make it available to remote employees after the meeting. I still felt awful. I apologized to the new CEO. I told him what had happened and acknowledged the mistake I made in assuming the connection was available. I told him about the workaround and assured him that all the remote employees would get his message, just not live. He was not happy. Neither was I.

A couple of hours after the meeting—after I'd gotten the recording available to all other employees—the new CEO called me to his office. He spent 10 minutes telling me how terrible it was that all the employees couldn't be on at the same time. He berated me for not double checking the Internet connection. He told me what I should do next time. Of course, these were all the same things I'd already told myself. He didn't tell me anything I didn't already know and there was no way I could have felt worse about it.

Application: *If you were to use this story, consider the following questions:*

What are the implications of the CEO berating someone for actions they already felt bad about?

What leadership lessons do you take from this story?

As written above, the story doesn't have a "here's the lesson" type of ending. How would you end the story to ensure it makes a point?

Job Description

Two years out of college, I was working my first "real" job—you know, one with a salary and benefits! I enjoyed the work and the team I worked with. We were in a time of change (pretty much a constant state in business), so I was taking on additional assignments than those in my job description.

During my annual review with my manager, I joked, "I think about 50 percent of my job now is 'Other duties as assigned.'" I didn't mind the additional work; I liked the variety and the opportunity to learn and grow.

My manager's response surprised me. She said, "You're right. I want you to rewrite your job description to reflect what you really do, then we'll send it to HR and see if we can reclassify your job."

Wow! What an opportunity! I get to write my own job description! What would you do with that opportunity? What would it mean to people who work for you if they could write their own job descriptions?

I took the task to heart and, over the next week, wrote a job description that reflected more accurately both the work I was doing and additional work I wanted to add to my position. I wrote, I edited, I pondered, I rewrote, until I had what I thought was a pretty strong job description. I left my masterpiece for the boss to review.

Two days later, the job description was back on my desk with a Post-It note in the boss's handwriting that said, "Come talk to me about this." Gulp! What did that mean? There wasn't a judgment, good or bad, and not even one editing mark on the paper. I wasn't sure what that meant, but it didn't seem good to me.

Later that day, I stopped by her office with the job description. She invited me to sit down and said, "It's got the right elements in it, but it's not strong enough. Instead of using words like "complete" or "work on" you need to use words like "lead" or "manage" or "direct." Put yourself in a position where you're taking more leadership on activities and it will get a higher grade level, which means a higher salary."

Not only did this change the way I thought about my job and the job description, but I've remembered that when preparing a résumé and interviewing for future jobs. It's more than just word choice, too. When we think about our work as "leading" and "directing" efforts, we have more ownership of the work we do and more passion for its success.

The next draft of my new job description had these stronger verbs in it. Oh, and the new job grade was *two levels higher* than the job I was working in.

Application: *If you were to use this story, consider the following questions:*

How can this story help you (or someone else) who is trying to expand their career?

What lessons do you learn from the way the manager handled this?

What are the lessons from the way the employee handled it?

Can you think of a "great boss" story of your own? What specifically did that boss do that you considered great? What lessons could you convey with your example of a "great boss"?

Play to Your Strengths

After working the first 10 years of my career in the communications department for a bank, I had a decision to make. I could become a banker and open myself up to other positions within the bank. Or I could stay at the same level of work I'd been in, which didn't sound attractive. Or I could change industries and expand my skills in a new direction.

I decided on option 3 and targeted a couple of different industries to pursue that were interesting to me: healthcare, education, and technology. This gets a little tricky. Any position that would be suitable for someone with 10 years of experience also included the line "industry background preferred" in the job description. How was I supposed to overcome that barrier without putting my career (and potentially income) in reverse for a while?

While interviewing for a public relations job at a technology company, the question of industry experience came up. The interviewer asked me, "You haven't had experience at a technology company. How can you overcome that lack of experience to be successful in this position?"

My response was, "I think that could be a benefit. As someone who doesn't have inside knowledge of your technology, I'll have to explain it in a way that our customers and others who are not inside the company will be able to understand. I'll be able to interpret the technology of the company in a way that the people we're trying to reach can relate to."

It's important to note that I wasn't saying that simply to get the job. I had thought this through and that's the answer I came to. The job of communications is to interpret the company to its key stakeholders. That job doesn't require an understanding of the software in the way an engineer would understand the software. It requires you to understand the technology in the way the end user wants to understand it—how the technology will help them and why that's important.

I got the job and worked in technology for the next 10 years, but more importantly, I learned that skills can be adapted to a variety of industries. Your job as an applicant is to make the connection clear between your skills—in whatever industry—and the job your potential employer needs done.

Application: *If you were to use this story, consider the following questions:*

How else could the concept of adapting skills to different jobs be applied?

How could this story be adapted to people looking for a promotion within the same company?

How could the idea of interpreting information to different audiences be helpful to those you teach or lead?

Know the Questions

The announcement came suddenly and unexpectedly: The company was selling off the products in our business unit and many of us would be without a job in three weeks. But keep working hard until further notice!

Sure enough, when the final cuts came, I was out of a job. I took the standard route to finding a new job—I told everyone I knew and started to look at job postings. But this all happened in December, the worst time of year to find a new job. Even if jobs are available, hiring managers are busy with year-end activities and priorities, so the interviews tend to slip to the first of the new year.

About this time, I happened upon a list of good questions for interviewers to ask prospective candidates. As part of my interview preparation, I studied those questions, wrote out my answers, then rehearsed my answers out loud. There were 21 questions on the list, and I had good answers for every one of them.

As I started interviewing, I noticed three things in relation to those questions and my answers. First, no one asked all 21 questions, but most interviewers asked at least some of them or some variation of them. Second, even when they didn't ask the questions on the list, my answers applied to other questions that came up. Third, having answers prepared gave me a high level of confidence going into job interviewers. Instead of wondering what they were going to ask and hoping I had a good answer, I shook hands with the interviewer confident that I had an answer for any question that came up.

I ended up getting a job at a slightly higher salary within a couple of months. But the more important result was the empowerment I felt in interviews.

I ran across those questions and my answers 20 years later. My answers to those questions today would be different, but faced with a similar situation, I would prepare in the same way.

Application: *If you want to use this story, consider the following questions:*

> How can this story relate to those looking for a new opportunity? How could it apply for those looking to advance internally?
>
> What key points of this story would you want to emphasize for yourself or others?
>
> What are some different ways you could use this story?

What experiences have you had when you took a slightly different approach and benefited from the change?

Lost Document; Lost Decorum

In a company of only 23 people, everyone hears everything. But on this particular day, the company could have been 223 people and everyone would have heard the CEO as he railed on the CFO in the hallway outside his office.

"What kind of idiot are you?" the CEO shouted. It was a rhetorical question. "You've just put our company at risk for ruin! If that document is in the wrong hands, we're done for, and you're the first one to go!"

The tirade went on for a full 90 seconds, but it seemed a lot longer. The outburst was punctuated by the slam of the CEO's office door. After that, the only sound you heard across the company was the hum of the air conditioner and the pitter-patter of fingers on keyboards—mostly likely messaging colleagues to find out what today's explosion was all about.

An hour later, the CEO's office door was still closed, so I ventured a visit to the CFO (who was a friend of mine) to see if he was okay. He was working on something at his desk, but I got the sense that it was busy work that didn't require much concentration. He looked up when I walked in.

"You okay?" I ventured. He nodded.

"What was that all about?" I asked.

He motioned for me to close the door. I shut it much softer than the CEO shut his.

"I ran some financial projections for the CEO last night," the CFO explained. "He wanted to see projections based on several different scenarios. I stayed late to get it done and left it for him on his desk. I was the last one out and locked the door behind me. But the document wasn't on his desk when he got in this morning. I have no idea what happened to it. I don't know what to do. He's right. If that information gets out, it could be terrible for us."

Justified or not, what do you imagine was the impact on the morale of the company by the CEO yelling at the CFO in the hallway of a small office space?

Two hours later, the CEO's door finally opened. He walked past the CFO's office without a word. The office was finally back to its normal level of chatter and noise.

Ten minutes later, the Chief Marketing Officer (CMO) poked his head into the CFO's office. "Hey, I just got back from a meeting," he said. "Do you know where the CEO is?"

The CFO shook his head. "No idea. He walked past here a few minutes ago, but I don't think he's talking to me anymore today."

The CMO asked why, and the CFO explained what had happened earlier, apparently while the CMO was at his meeting. As the CFO got deeper into the story, the CMO started looking chagrined. "Hold on," he said, and walked away.

Seconds later he returned with the financial report in his hand. "I came in early this morning and noticed the report on the CEO's desk. This is exactly the kind of information I needed to make some marketing projections the CEO asked for, so I borrowed the report. I didn't think he'd miss it before I was back from the meeting."

The CFO asked the CMO to explain that to the CEO when he returned the report, which he did. What would you expect the CEO to do once he got that new information?

What the CEO actually did was ... nothing. He never mentioned it again, publicly or privately. He acted as if nothing had happened.

Again, what do you imagine the impact was on everyone else at the company when the CEO failed to acknowledge his error? In a company of 23 people, everyone knew that there was not even a private apology. In this instance, the CEO took one mistake and made it into two.

Application: *If you want to use this story, consider the following questions:*

This is an extreme example of someone publicly ridiculing a team member. How does this happen in more subtle ways? What does it look like?

When we make mistakes, how do we best recover from them?

What could the CEO have done to prevent this problem? What could the CFO have done differently?

What is the impact in your organization when people treat others disrespectfully?

Endnotes:
Citations and Other Confessions

Chapter 1

1. Rob Walker and Josh Glenn: http://significantobjects.com/about/ accessed 8.31.17. What a fascinating experiment! If you weren't persuaded before that stories are powerful, this should do it.

2. Dan Ariely: http://danariely.com/2009/12/25/the-significant-objects-project/ Ariely is one of our favorite social scientists. He has a compelling personal story that rolls right into his fascinating work.

3. Shankar Vedantam: *Hidden Brain* podcast, "Alan Alda Wants us to Have Better Conversations" 1.22.18. *Hidden Brain* is interesting. Alan Alda is interesting. Our brains are interesting. That's a trifecta.

4. Paul Zak: *Trust Factor*. We're so glad Dr. Zak persuaded numerous people to let him draw their blood under varied circumstances so we can better understand the science behind storytelling. See also, "Why Your Brain Loves Good Storytelling" a *Harvard Business Review* digital article published October 28, 2014.

5. Giacomo Rizzolatti: See https://www.youtube.com/watch?v=yKPTuCoop8c for an introduction to Dr. Rizzolatti's work. As a bonus, enjoy his charming Italian accent.

6. Marco Iacoboni: For example, see https://www.scientificamerican.com/article/the-mirror-neuron-revolut/# and https://www.youtube.com/watch?v=ESM7b-X8zhQ.

Dr. Iacoboni was also kind enough to answer specific questions via email. He, too, has a charming Italian accent, but it gets lost in email; his English is too good.

7. Patti Digh: TEDx Indiana talk: https://www.youtube.com/watch?v=3hVReRJCTHU @ 5:28. What a great one-liner.

8. Joseph Grenny: "Great Storytelling Connects Employees to Their Work," *HBR online*, 9.25.17: https://hbr.org/2017/09/great-storytelling-connects-employees-to-their-work. Joseph is a long-time mentor of ours (which is why we get to call him by his first name), and we never cease to be enthralled by his intelligent and impactful work.

9. Teresa Amabile and Steven J. Kramer: https://hbr.org/2011/05/the-power-of-small-wins; Timothy A. Pychyl: https://www.psychologytoday.com/us/blog/dont-delay/200806/goal-progress-and-happiness. Sometimes, small is big — or at least it leads to big.

10. Harrison Monarth: "The Irresistible Power of Storytelling as a Strategic Business Tool," *Harvard Business Review*, 3.11.14: https://hbr.org/2014/03/the-irresistible-power-of-storytelling-as-a-strategic-business-tool. This is the argument we make throughout this book. We're trying to make the idea accessible to everyone, not just advertisers, med students, and trial lawyers. And we promise we had the idea for the book before we read the article. (Monarth quotes Paul Zak, too!)

Chapter 2

1. Shawn Achor: *The Happiness Advantage*. This is a great book, and if you haven't yet joined the millions who have viewed his TED talk, you have a delightful 12-minute journey awaiting you: https://www.youtube.com/watch?v=fLJsdqxnZb0.

Chapter 3

The only authority we cite in this chapter is experience. While we like to quote other people — and we've learned a ton from them — we've also learned a thing or two ourselves.

Chapter 4

1. Malcolm Gladwell: https://www.youtube.com/watch?v=E0RDJ9tYw6A @ 1:06. Gladwell is enlightening even in infomercials!

Chapter 5

1. Anthony G. Greenwald, Catherine G. Carnot, Rebecca Beach, and Barbara Young: https://www.researchgate.net/publication/232579629_Increasing_Voting_Behavior_by_Asking_People_If_They_Expect_to_Vote; Godin G, Sheeran P, Conner M, Germain M.: https://www.ncbi.nlm.nih.gov/pubmed/18377136; Patti Williams, Lauren G. Block, and Gavan J. Fitzsimons: https://faculty.fuqua.duke.edu/%7Egavan/bio/GJF_articles/asking_about_drugs_social_influence_2006.pdf The point is that asking questions to get people to *envision* their future behavior is far more powerful than merely asking them to *predict* their behavior.

2. Not convinced that you cannot focus on more than one thing at a time? Just type in "myth of multitasking" in

Google or YouTube and see how many sources share the science behind this claim.

3. Bloom, B. S.; Engelhart, M. D.; Furst, E. J.; Hill, W. H.; Krathwohl, D. R.: *Taxonomy of Educational Objectives, The Classification of Educational Goals, Handbook 1: Cognitive Domain*, 1956/1984. This was a watershed work. Successors have enhanced the original and made it easier to use. If you're a teacher or trainer, you should master at least the basics of Bloom's Taxonomy.

Chapter 6

1. Noah Zandan: "How to Stop Saying 'Um,' 'Ah,' and 'You Know'" in *Harvard Business Review*, August 1, 2018. As you can see, we like *HBR*. There are several other great articles on the power of storytelling in its volumes. You ought to consider a subscription. (That's an unpaid endorsement.)

2. *ibid*. While we did like this article, we cite it twice just so we could use a Latin abbreviation in our book. Fun fact: *ibidem* (the full word) means "in the same place — used to indicate that a reference is from the same source as a previous reference." (Merriam-Webster online)

3. Ron McMillan: For the life of me, I can't find the podcast I heard Ron say this on. But I didn't imagine it, and I know it was Ron. As a sign that he forgives us, he did the terrific forward to this book. (Ron's another mentor of ours.

Who Are These Guys?

"Master Mark" Carpenter is a one-man story dispensary. The story you read at the beginning of chapter three ("You Can Find Stories ...") is classic Mark: He really does have a story for everything! That's because he's full of life — enthusiastic, observant, and bright. I think he's been honing his storytelling craft for years preparing for his favorite role: grandpa. But to me, he is "Mark the Muse" inspiring me to be my best — and knowing just when and how to light a (friendly) fire under me to get the job done. He matches a vibrant work ethic with an equally intense passion for helping people get better. He's a true friend, a consummate professional, and a talented communicator, on the page and in person.

By Darrell Harmon

Here's what you need to know about **Darrell Harmon** — and it's not all that bio stuff like his MBA, organizational development background, consulting practice, and coaching prowess. What you need to know is that he's super smart. All the words in this book that you had to use a dictionary to understand, Darrell added those (he threw a few of them into my sections to try to make me look smarter). He even speaks fluent Italian (well beyond my vocabulary of *ciao* and *gelato*). Darrell is clear thinking and level-headed; I don't ever remember seeing him get flustered. That's what makes him an effective referee for high school basketball games. Most important, he's a loving father and husband and a loyal friend.

By Mark Carpenter

Want More?

We hope you've enjoyed this short stroll through the land of turning experiences into stories that effectively teach, lead, and inspire. We also recognize it may not be possible to get everything you need from a book (as good as that book may be).

If you want to ramp up your storytelling superpower, here are a few options:

1) Check out our free resources at www.Master-Storytelling.com. We referenced this is the book's text, but here's a reminder. We have a Story Catcher worksheet that will help you craft your experiences into effective stories.

2) Attend our Master Storytelling workshop. You'll go deeper into the power of storytelling and walk away with at least two experiences that you've turned into stories you'll be able to use right away. The workshop is available in person or virtually. We even have an on-demand version Go to the website for more information: www.Master-Storytelling.com/events/.

3) Sign up for storytelling coaching. If you want more personal attention, look into our storytelling coaching options. We can do virtual or in-person coaching. Wondering where to go for information? You got it: www.Master-Storytelling.com.

We'd also love your feedback. Drop us an email at Info@Master-Storytelling.com.